Communications in Computer and Information Science 565

Commenced Publication in 2007
Founding and Former Series Editors:
Alfredo Cuzzocrea, Dominik Ślęzak, and Xiaokang Yang

More information about this series at http://www.springer.com/series/7899

Carla Osthoff · Philippe Olivier Alexandre Navaux
Carlos Jaime Barrios Hernandez
Pedro L. Silva Dias (Eds.)

High Performance Computing

Second Latin American Conference, CARLA 2015
Petrópolis, Brazil, August 26–28, 2015
Proceedings

 Springer

Editors
Carla Osthoff
LNCC
National Laboratory for Scientific
  Computing
Rio de Janeiro
Brazil

Philippe Olivier Alexandre Navaux
Instituto de Informática
Universidade Federal do Rio Grande do Su
Porto Alegre
Brazil

Carlos Jaime Barrios Hernandez
High Performance and Scientific Computing
Universidad Industrial de Santander
Bucaramanga
Chile

Pedro L. Silva Dias
LNCC
National Laboratory for Scientific
  Computing
Rio de Janeiro
Brazil

ISSN 1865-0929   ISSN 1865-0937   (electronic)
Communications in Computer and Information Science
ISBN 978-3-319-26927-6   ISBN 978-3-319-26928-3   (eBook)
DOI 10.1007/978-3-319-26928-3

Library of Congress Control Number: 2015940735

Springer Cham Heidelberg New York Dordrecht London
© Springer International Publishing Switzerland 2015

Printed on acid-free paper

Springer International Publishing AG Switzerland is part of Springer Science+Business Media
(www.springer.com)

Preface

The Latin American High-Performance Computing Conference, CARLA (http://www.ccarla.org) is a joint conference of the High-Performance Computing Latin America Community – HPCLATAM – and the Conferencia Latino Americana de Computación de Alto Rendimiento – CLCAR. In 2015 both major HPC Latin-American workshops joined again in CARLA 2015, and were held at the Laboratório Nacional de Computação Científica (http://www.lncc.br), in Petrópolis, Brazil.

HPCLATAM (http://hpclatam.org) gathers a young but growing community of scientists and practitioners in the HPC area in Latin America. The past events proved that the HPC community in the region is steadily growing. HPCLATAM aims to bring together researchers, developers, and users of HPC to discuss new ideas, experiences, and problems. The main goal of HPCLATAM is to provide a regional forum fostering the growth of the HPC community in Latin America through the exchange and dissemination of new ideas, techniques, and research in HPC.

The CLCAR (http://www.cenat.ac.cr/) conference has been held since 2007 and is driven by a group of researchers from universities and research centers in Latin America that seek to promote a space for discussion of new knowledge and trends in the area. A further aim is to coordinate initiatives and efforts toward the development of technologies for high-performance computing that can contribute to solving common problems of social and economic relevance to the region. CLCAR is an event for students and scientists and is dedicated to the areas of high-performance computing, parallel and distributed systems, e-science and its applications to real-life problems, but especially focused on Latin American researchers.

The CARLA 2015 symposium featured invited talks from academy and industry speakers, with short- and full-paper sessions presenting both mature work and new ideas in research and industrial applications in HPC. This conference was co-located with the First Rio de Janeiro High-Performance Computing School – ERAD-RJ 2015 (http://eradrj2015.lncc.br) – held during August 24–25, 2015, and the Second HPCAC Brazil Conference (http://hpcadvisorycouncil.com/events/2015/brazil-workshop), held August 26, 2015.

Topics of interest from this edition include:

- Scientific Computing Applications
- GPU and MIC Computing: Methods, Libraries and Applications
- Grid and Cloud Computing

The CARLA 2015 website (http://www.ccarla.org) provides access to the talks at the meetings and to photos of the activities. The website (http://www.ccarla.org) also gives information on the latest event. This book contains the best papers from CARLA 2015, including ten technical papers. The paper by Aline Paes and Daniel Oliveira,

"Running Multi-relational Data Mining Processes in the Cloud: A Practical Approach for Social Networks," was selected for the Best Paper Award. All technical papers were peer reviewed by at least three different members of the Program Committee.

October 2015

Carla Osthoff
Philippe Olivier Alexandre Navaux
Carlos Jaime Barrios Hernandez
Pedro L. Silva Dias

Organization

General Chair

Pedro L. Silva Dias   LNCC, Laboratório Nacional de Computação Cientifica, Brazil

Co-chairs

Carlos Jaime Barrios   Universidad Industrial de Santander, Colombia
Gonzalo Hernandez   Universidad Técnica Federico Santa Maria, Chile
Wagner Meira   Universidade Federal de Minas Gerais, Brazil
Carla Osthoff   Laboratório Nacional de Computação Cientifica, Brazil
Alvaro Coutinho   Universidade Federal do Rio de Janeiro, Brazil
Phillippe Navaux   Universidade Federal do Rio Grande do Sul, Brazil

Technical Program Committee

Tracks Coordinators

GPU and MIC Computing

Nicolás Wolowick   Universidad Nacional de Córdoba, Argentina
Esteban Clua   Universidade Federal Fluminense, Brazil

Grid and Cloud Computing

Carlos García-Garino   Universidad Nacional de Cuyo, Argentina
Francisco Brasileiro   Universidade Federal de Campina Grande, Brazil

Scientific Computing and Computing Applications

Isidoro Gitler   CINVESTAV, México

Technical Program Committee Members

Carlos Couder Castañeda   CINVESTAV, México
Russlan Gobassov   Autonomous University of Hidalgo, Mexico
Emmanuel Nicolas Millan   Universidad Nacional de Cuyo, Argentina
Nirvana Belen Caballero   Universidad Nacional de Córdoba, Argentina
Marcelo Zamith   Universidade Rural do Rio de Janeiro, Brazil

Contents

Scientific Computing Applications

Grid and Cloud Computing

Running Multi-relational Data Mining Processes in the Cloud: A Practical Approach for Social Networks

Aline Paes and Daniel de Oliveira[✉]

Instituto de Computação, Universidade Federal Fluminense – IC/UFF,
Niterói, Brazil
{alinepaes, danielcmo}@ic.uff.br

Abstract. Multi-relational Data Mining algorithms (MRDM) are the appropriate approach for inferring knowledge from databases containing multiple relationships between non-homogenous entities, which are precisely the case of datasets obtained from social networks. However, to acquire such expressivity, the search space of candidate hypotheses in MRDM algorithms is more complex than those obtained from traditional data mining algorithms. To allow a feasible search space of hypotheses, MRDM algorithms adopt several language biases during the mining process. Because of that, when running a MRDM-based system, the user needs to execute the same set of data mining tasks a number of times, each assuming a different combination of parameters in order to get a final good hypothesis. This makes manual control of such complex process tedious, laborious and error-prone. In addition, running the same MRDM process several times consumes much time. Thus, the automatic execution of each setting of parameters throughout parallelization techniques becomes essential. In this paper, we propose an approach named LPFlow4SN that models a MRDM process as a scientific workflow and then executes it in parallel in the cloud, thus benefiting from the existing Scientific Workflow Management Systems. Experimental results reinforce the potential of running parallel scientific workflows in the cloud to automatically control the MRDM process while improving its overall execution performance.

1 Introduction

Social networks technologies have enabled the insertion of new practices in our society [1]. By using social networks, their members are allowed to exchange information, promote events and debates, *etc.* [1]. However, there is some information about the social networks that is not always directly, such as how an individual connects to another one. Let us consider as an example a social network composed of students, professors, projects and courses of a university as proposed by Richardson and Domingos [2]. Each one of these entities has properties to specialize them, such as "a course is advanced, intermediary or basic". Also, they may have a relationship with each other, for example, "a professor teaches a course in a specific semester". Now, suppose we need to find out which professors are advising students starting from these properties and relationships, a task known as link prediction [32]. Through the data we

C. Osthoff et al. (Eds.): CARLA 2015, CCIS 565, pp. 3–18, 2015.
DOI: 10.1007/978-3-319-26928-3_1

can find out that "if a professor X taughts a course C in the semester Q, C is a graduation course and Y is a research assistant of X in the course, then Y is advised by X". As the dataset is composed of several instances of entities, their properties and relationships, it is not trivial to manually discover this conceptualization of relationships. To automatically achieve this we need data mining algorithms [3].

However, there is a problem in using the traditional data mining algorithms for analyzing structures such as social networks. Traditional data mining algorithms assume that data is homogeneous, independent of each other and described in the attribute-value form [3–6]. Since data obtained from social networks is commonly multi-related, structured and sampled from complex relationships (*e.g.*, the aforementioned example of professor-student social network), using traditional data mining algorithms on them is not feasible, as they fail to correctly capture and describe how individuals in social networks are related.

On the other hand, the research area of Multi-Relational Data Mining [7, 8] (*i.e.*, MRDM) aims at automatically inducing hypotheses from data arranged in multiple related tables. Thus, MRDM algorithms are quite adequate to discover patterns and describe characteristics of relationships embedded in social networks, for example. In this context, the area of Inductive Logic Programming (ILP) [8–10] is attracting a lot of attention for running complex MRDM analyses, being the intersection of machine learning and knowledge representation. In ILP, the hypotheses are induced in the format of logic programs and thus benefit from the power of expressivity of First-Order Logic [11]. In addition to the examples, a preliminary knowledge about the problem, known as background knowledge, described in first-order logic language, can also be provided as input to the ILP algorithms.

However, to infer expressive and refined hypotheses, ILP algorithms take into account complex search spaces and strategies for induction, which are usually less computationally efficient than those used in traditional data mining approaches. In ILP, for example, the hypothesis refinement requires logical proof of the examples from the current hypothesis and the informed preliminary knowledge [8–10]. Thus, to reduce the space of possible hypotheses to be refined, it is necessary to provide bias to the language and to the algorithm refinement process. These inputs and parameters are not trivially defined, which makes important to try several values for the many different combination of parameters involved in the entire analysis.

Each combination of parameter values has to be tested in the MRDM process. Once all possible values for the parameters have been evaluated, we have a higher probability that good hypotheses are obtained. However, as the evaluation of all possible combinations of parameter values tends to be a computing intensive and error-prone task (if performed manually), analysts commonly choose not to evaluate all possible combinations. This simplification introduces a risk to the analysis process as a whole, since valid and important results are commonly discarded. This way, data mining analysts need an infrastructure that allows them to automatically and systematically execute all possible combinations of parameters in a feasible time.

Over the last decade, the e-science community has been working on techniques for modeling and managing a coherent flow of scientific programs, the well-known concept of scientific workflows [12–14]. Since a MRMD process is composed by several applications with a certain data dependency among them, it is intuitive that we can model a MRMD process as a scientific workflow and benefit from the facilities already provided by existing Scientific Workflow Management Systems (SWfMS). In fact, modeling a traditional data mining process was already proposed [15] (without considering MRDM and parallelism issues). Many of these SWfMS include support for parallel executions in High Performance Computing (HPC) environments such as HPC clouds, which can provide the MRDM analyst the opportunity to explore all possible combinations of parameters in a feasible time by executing tasks in parallel using several virtual machines. Additionally, SWfMSs provide the so-called data provenance [16, 17] that record a complete execution history of the workflow. This provenance data is useful for the data-mining analyst to perform a *post-mortem* analysis of their MRDM process, including validating the results. Thus, we can use scientific workflows systems and techniques as a way to improve the management of MRDM knowledge discovery process.

However, too much effort may be needed for MRDM analysts to model a scientific workflow. Substantial expertise may be required to install and configure the several dependent software programs and the data dependencies among them. Thus, a solution that empowers and integrates parallel execution of the workflow and MRDM analysts is needed to bridge this gap. In this context, this paper presents LPFlow4SN, a scientific workflow deployed in the cloud that allows managing the parallel execution of a MRDM workflow based on ILP algorithms. LPFlow4SN is modeled on the top of SciCumulus workflow system [18–20] and it is deployed on the Amazon EC2 environment[1]. Using this approach, the MRDM analyst does not have to worry about modeling the analysis process as a workflow. Instead, he/she should only inform the dataset to be used. The proposed approach checks which combinations of parameters must be processed within an ILP system and then executes the entire process into multiple virtual machines in parallel in the cloud. To the best of our knowledge, this is the first approach capable of performing experiments with multi-relational data represented in logic using scientific workflows.

This paper is organized into four sections besides this introduction. Section 2 presents a conceptual survey of scientific workflows and inductive logic programming. Section 3 presents the proposed approach. Section 4 presents the case study performed with LPFlow4SN. Finally, Sect. 5 concludes this paper and points out future work.

2 Background Knowledge

Inductive Logic Programming. Traditional data mining algorithms usually processes information expressed in a format of propositional representation in the sense that they search for patterns from homogeneous data sampled from simple relations [3]. However, data from social networks and many other domains contain multiple entities, typically arranged in several related tables. The Inductive Logic Programming is a subarea of Machine Learning [21], which enables mining of multi-relational data by

---

[1] http://aws.amazon.com/.

combining machine learning techniques and knowledge representation to induce expressive hypotheses described as logic programs.

An ILP system receives as input a set of examples, divided into positive examples and negative examples, a background knowledge (BK) and a set of parameters that specify the language and constrain the search space of a hypothesis. To exemplify, let us consider the same scenario presented in the introduction: a social network of students, professors and employees of a university [2]. Other entities in this domain are the projects developed in the university; the courses taught and associated publications, *among others.* A typical relationship that can be explained within this context is the advising relation, represented by the logical predicate *advisedBy.* Thus, the positive samples would be well-known examples of such a relationship, whereas the negative examples would be examples of individuals who are not part of such a relationship. Assuming, for example, that *person1* is a student and a professor *person10* advises *person1,* we would have the literal *advisedBy(person1, person10) as a positive example.* On the other hand, a negative example could be *advisedBy(person11, person10),* whereas *person11* is not advised by *person10.* Background knowledge consists of facts and logic clauses [11] that show properties and characteristics of the individuals in the domain, as well as previously known rules of regularity. In the aforementioned example, the BK could contain a logical fact *projectMember(project1, person10),* which specifies that *person10* participates in *project1.* An example of a logic clause in this context could be: *courseLevel(C, basiclevel):- ta(C,S,Q), inPhase(S,pre_Quals), student(s), course(C).* This logic clause can be read in natural language as follows: "if *S* was a teaching assistant in the course *C* in the semester *Q,* *S* is in the pre-qualification phase, *S* is a student and *C* is a course, then *C* is a basic level course". Note that *C* and *S* are variables that can be replaced by any instances of entities in the domain, but as soon as they are replaced by a specific individual in any literal of the rule, another individual in another literal of the same rule cannot replace it.

The output of an ILP system is a logical program composed of clauses in first-order logic. In the domain exemplified above, the ILP system could induce the following rule from the set of examples and BK: *advisedBy(S,P):- taughtBy(C,P,Q), courseLevel (C,graduateLevel), ta(C,S,Q).* This indicates that if a professor teaches a postgraduate course and there is a teaching assistant, the professor advises the teaching assistant.

Scientific Workflows and Provenance Data. Scientific workflows are an attractive alternative to represent the coherent flow of programs instead of using an *ad-hoc* approach based on scripts or manual executions [12]. In the context of this paper, a scientific workflow may be seen as one of the trials conducted in the context of a MRDM analysis to evaluate a specific hypothesis. The set of trials represented by each distinct workflow execution defines one single MRDM analysis. Scientific workflows can be defined as an abstraction for modelling the flow of activities and data. These activities are usually programs or services that represent algorithms and robust computational methods [12]. Such workflows are managed by complex systems called Scientific Workflow Management Systems (SWfMS) [13]. There are several SWfMS, each one with a main feature as support for visualization, ontologies or parallelism mechanisms. As the complexity of the scientific workflow grows (*e.g.,* exploration of thousands of parameters and in many cases using repetition structures over dozens of complex activities), running scientific workflows demands parallelism and powerful HPC capabilities that can be provided by several types of HPC environments such as clusters and grids. In 2008, the paradigm of Many Tasks Computing (MTC) was proposed by Raicu et al. [22] to solve the problem of executing multiple parallel tasks in multiple processors. This paradigm consists on several computing resources used over short periods of time to accomplish many computational tasks, which is exactly the case of MRDM processes where each combination of parameter values executes over shorts periods of time. Due to the move of scientific experiments to clouds and increasing demands of those experiments for parallelization, executing parallel scientific workflows in clouds is already provided by several SWfMS [18, 23, 24]. Although clouds provide elastic resources that can be used to execute parallel instances of a specific scientific workflow, in the cloud the SWfMS has to manage some new important aspects such as initialization of virtualized instances, scheduling workflow activities over different virtual machines, impact of data, *etc.*

Besides parallelism capabilities, one of the main advantages of SWfMS is to manage the experiment metadata, called data provenance [16, 17]. Data provenance records the origin and the history of information in a scientific experiment and it is essential to the reproducibility and evaluation of results. Thus, Freire *et al.* define the term as a description of the origin of a given object and the process by which it arrived in a database. This metadata is fundamental for MRDM analyses because in the same analysis, the workflow can be executed n times only varying its parameters. For example, in a MRDM process a critical component of the refinement process of a hypothesis is the optimization function used to score the candidate hypotheses. Commonly, the optimization function used is based on the coverage of examples, *i.e.*, it takes into account the amount of positive examples correctly inferred by the candidate hypothesis, and the amount of negative incorrectly inferred. However, if the training base is unbalanced, *i.e.*, if there are many more negative examples than positive (or *vice-versa*), this function will lead to the proposal of a very specific hypothesis, that proves only a few examples. This seems good considering the large number of negative examples. However, a downside is that only a few positive examples are going to be correctly classified. Usually, social networks generate unbalanced datasets, as the number of not-connected individuals is much larger than the individuals actually connected to each other. In such cases, the optimization functions that give more importance to correctly classified positive examples than to the overall coverage, as the F-measure [25], are more appropriate. It is essential to know exactly what outcome is associated with which evaluation measure in the analysis, even to disregard in future analyses that have the same characteristics of the current analysis when the functions do not produce good hypotheses.

Today, the MRDM analyst commonly performs all these executions and analysis processes manually, *which is time consuming and* error-prone. A systematic process of using scientific workflows is a solution with many advantages, such as the specification of the tacit knowledge of the MRDM process and possibility of running MRDM analyses in parallel in HPC environments to produce results in a viable time. For this, we should use an SWfMS that provides parallelism capabilities in HPC environments allied to provenance capture and management. However, to model a scientific workflow in existing SWfMS requires some expertise and it is not a trivial task to be performed. This way, we propose a scientific workflow named LPFlow4SN that allows for MRDM analysts to execute their analyses using an SWfMS that does not require much effort from the analyst.

3 A Cloud-Based Approach for Running MRDM Analysis in Parallel

In this section, we present the LPFlow4SN workflow that is implemented based on the SWfMS SciCumulus and a MRDM process proposed for social network analysis.

SciCumulus Workflow System. SciCumulus[2] is a workflow system that manages the parallel execution of scientific workflows in cloud environments, such as Amazon EC2 or Microsoft Azure. Based on the workflow specification and the input datasets provided by scientists, SciCumulus is able to distribute activity executions (that we call activations [26]) on a set of virtual machines, mapping data to these activations, thus increasing parallelism. It has a 3-objective weighted cost model [19] where scientists can inform their preferences for scheduling activations: they can focus on minimizing the incidence of errors (α_2), minimizing execution time (α_1) or minimizing financial costs (α_3). This way, SciCumulus distributes the activations according to its estimated execution time or predicted failure rate to the most suitable virtual machine that is idle at the moment. Differently from many workflow systems, SciCumulus executes workflows in static or adaptive modes [19]. In the adaptive mode, SciCumulus is able to perform a horizontal scaling to overcome problems on the environment or to meet scientists' deadlines such as max execution time or max allowed financial cost. SciCumulus is able to add (or remove) virtual machines from the pool of available virtual machines during the workflow execution. Since MRDM workflows process hundreds or even thousands of input files, HPC adaptive mechanisms are likely to be essential to provide scalability.

For monitoring, SciCumulus has a notification mechanism that identifies pre-defined events, through queries on provenance data generated at runtime. Notification is a relevant alternative for long-term "black-box" executions since it is unviable for scientists to stay at a monitor for several hours or even days. Scientists may define preconfigured events to be notified. Since MRDM workflows can execute for several hours or days and produce a large variety of events (errors, activity termination, *etc.*), monitoring mechanisms are effectively required and were used.

For the analysis of the results, SciCumulus provenance repository provides fine-grained information about the experiment and the cloud environment. Statistics on previous executions of scientific workflows are obtained by querying this database. Provenance data is also the input to the cost model, to estimate the execution time and adapt the scheduling. Execution information of the provenance model is captured at each virtual machine involved in the execution and from the cloud environment. This provenance repository follows the PROV-Wf [27] recommendation and contains information about elements that represent: (i) MRDM processes executed in the cloud;

---

[2] Download SciCumulus at: https://scicumulusc2.wordpress.com/.

(ii) files consumed and produced by the workflow execution, (iii) the temporality of data and (*i.e.,* when data is produced and consumed), (iv) information about the cloud environment (*e.g.,* number of VMs, IPs, amount of RAM, amount of disk, *etc.*). Besides reproducibility, the provenance repository of SciCumulus allows for monitoring, fault-tolerance and adaptation of the workflow execution, which is in sync with requirements defined by the top researchers in the community as stressed by Ailamaki *et al.* [28].

Modeling the MRDM Process as a Scientific Workflow. Different executions of the hypotheses discovery in social networks using MRDM algorithms require specific processes to constrain the language and to reduce the search space when finding the best hypothesis parameters. As in the life cycle of a traditional scientific experiment [12], the MRDM analyst should perform all stages of a MRDM process in a controlled manner. The power of expression obtained with MRDM algorithms and systems comes with complex search spaces. For the process to be viable then becomes necessary to define parameters guiding the search space of hypotheses. A specific combination of parameters may cause the MRDM process to return hypotheses that are more accurate (or not). However, there is not a set of parameters that can be effectively used to any domain and finding the best combination to use (or at least a good enough combination), is far from trivial. Thus, although the idea behind the workflow presented in this section may be considered simple, it requires a high computational power, because there maybe hundreds or even thousands combinations of parameters to be evaluated before returning the final hypothesis to the analyst. In addition to the various combinations of parameters to be explored, to minimize the possibility of overfitting the hypothesis, the experimental process in data mining makes use of the mechanism of cross-validation [3]. In cross-validation, the input dataset is divided into k partitions and the experimental procedure is performed k times. Although this mechanism is essential to produce hypotheses that generalize the set of examples, its usage introduces an additional element of complexity in the experimental process, since each iteration of the MRDM process is performed k times. By modeling the process as a workflow and executing it using a workflow system such as SciCumulus, the hypothesis induction guided by each configuration of parameters can be performed in parallel on multiple virtual machines in the cloud, reducing the total execution time of the workflow (and often making it feasible).

In the proposed and developed workflow, the used MRDM system was Aleph (**A** **L**earning **E**ngine for **P**roposing **H**ypothesis) [10]. The Aleph system was originally developed to induce hypotheses using the paradigm of inverse resolution, but in the last years, it evolved to emulate several other ILP algorithms.. Due to this fact, Aleph is currently the most used system for implementing and validating new algorithms developed in the area of ILP. Moreover, as its code is free and open source, the Aleph is a *de facto* system for development and exploration of new MRDM approaches. All these reasons make the Aleph system ideal for composing the workflow proposed and analyzed in this paper. To run Aleph we need YAP which is a Prolog compiler. The input provided to the Aleph system is organized in three Prolog files: (i) a file with the extension *.f* containing the positive examples; (ii) a file with the extension *.n* that contains negative examples and (iii) a file with the extension *.b* containing the background knowledge of facts and/or rules, restrictions of the language and of the search space and any other directives understood by a Prolog interpreter. All information contained in this latest file can also be transferred directly to the Prolog interpreter via parameters.

The Aleph system has several parameters that must be explored in order to find results with good accuracy. For example, Aleph assumes by default that the maximum size of a rule is 5 literals. However, in ILP, larger clauses may generate hypotheses that are more specific and therefore covering less negative examples. Thus, in some areas, it may be useful to generate more than 5 clauses literals, but we have to set a maximum size so that the inference is not too computational costly. With *clauselength* parameter is possible to set this maximum size. Again, different problems may require clauses with different maximum sizes. Another parameter that may influence the induction of rules is the one that defines the optimization function to be used during the search, called *evalfn*. Some possible values for this parameter are *coverage,* which tries to improve the coverage of positive examples while not covering negative examples; *accuracy*, which prefers hypothesis that maximizing the number of correctly classified examples. Another example that typically generates very diverse hypotheses is the *noise* parameter, whose function is to establish a maximum negative to be covered by a clause, so that a clause does not become too specific. The Aleph system accommodates many other variations of parameters. For a complete description of the parameters, please refer to the Aleph manual[3].

Thus, we used the Aleph system to develop the LPFlow4SN workflow. The workflow presented in Fig. 1 allows for any combination of values of any parameters. To allow an extensive experimental process, exploring all the possibilities of the Aleph

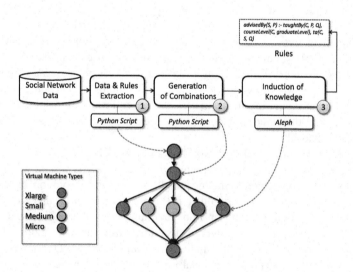

Fig. 1. Conceptual definition of the MRDM workflow

---

[3] http://web.comlab.ox.ac.uk/oucl/research/areas/machlearn/Aleph/aleph.html.

configuration, the proposed workflow associates an activation to each combination of parameters values. The workflow consists of three activities as presented in Fig. 1.

The first activity of the workflow (*Data and Rules Extraction*) aims at generating the configuration files to be used in MRDM approach (for Aleph). This activity is implemented by a Python script that "crawls" the structure of the social network, identifies and extracts the positive examples, negative examples and the background knowledge. Importantly, this script must be customized for each type of social network to be analyzed. For example, data from Facebook™ are different from Twitter™. After this extraction, the script sets this information in the facts and/or rules so that a Prolog interpreter can process them. The workflow system should not perform this activity in parallel because this activity is not computing intensive. The second activity of the workflow is the activity responsible for generating parameter combinations. With the information produced by the first activity, the second activity (*Generation of Combinations*) examines which parameters should be explored and what are the possible values associated with them. For each combination of parameter values, the workflow system should generate an activation to be executed in parallel in the third activity (*induction of knowledge*). In the third activity, the Aleph framework is invoked on multiple virtual machines in parallel where each machine performs a combination of different parameter values. In the example of Fig. 1, each type of virtual machine (according to the existing virtual machine types in Amazon EC2) is displayed in a different color. Thus, the first two activities are not parallelized and run on the m3. xlarge virtual machine. The third activity is amenable to parallelization and runs on m3. xlarge, m1.medium, m1.small, and t1.micro virtual machines, where each consumes a combination of parameter values.

In the context of this paper, the workflow was modeled and executed using SciCumulus workflow system. SciCumulus receives a workflow modeled by the user (in a XML format), transforms it into algebraic expressions (following the workflow algebra proposed by Ogasawara *et al.* [26]), generates an workflow execution plan and, while executing the workflow, it represents all data involved in the execution as relations and relationships in a database. This way, each combination of parameter values to be consumed by each activity of the workflow is represented in tables in the database as presented in Fig. 2.

As presented in Fig. 2, the first activity consumes only the parameters *namedataset* and *path*. The first one represents the name of the dataset to be processed and the latter the path where it can be accessed or downloaded. Since there is only one tuple in the table (where the dataset name is *uwcse*) only one activation is generated and executed. When this activation has been executed and the dataset was converted into Prolog rules, the second activity is performed. The second activity then creates several tuples in the database to perform the cross-validation. Each tuple is associated with an activation. This way, after execution of the second activity, all combinations of parameter values are generated to be processed in the third activity. All parameters values in SciCumulus are stored in a relational database, which makes SciCumulus a provenance-oriented workflow system. A partial extraction of the tables involved in a workflow execution with SciCumulus can be viewed in Fig. 2. In addition, in Fig. 2 the colored circle near to each row of the table indicate which virtual machine processed the combination of parameter values.

Thus, for the analyst to define the workflow in SciCumulus, he/she should create an XML file format that can be parsed by SciCumulus. In this XML file, we need to inform the workflow configuration parameters and environment, *e.g.*, the database where data will be stored. Another important parameter is the workflow tag that registers the name of the workflow run and defines its activities. Each activity has a workflow Activity tag associated with their input relations (Relation), which are composed of parameters (Field). With the modeled XML in hands, the analyst can now run the LPFlow4SN workflow and analyze their results.

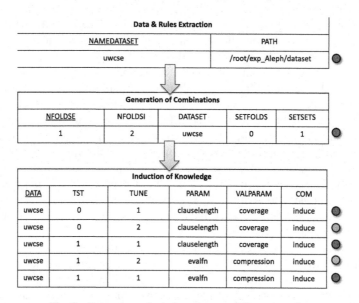

Fig. 2. Extraction of relations in a workflow execution

4 Experimental Evaluation

This section presents the results obtained from the performance evaluation of the analysis of an academic social network with the proposed LPFlow4SN workflow. We used the social network composed by the advising relationship between students and professors in the Department of Computer Science at the University of Washington, presented in the introduction. The advising relationship (or lack of it) leads to the positive (or negative) examples, represented by the *advisedby* predicate. When there is more than one entity involved, we have a relationship. When only one entity is listed, we have a property associated with that entity. The used database contains 114 positive examples and 2,438 negative examples, 5,058 facts without logical variables associated within 10 predicates. These predicates are other relationships between entities professors, courses, students and academic semesters, as well as properties of entities, such as the position of a professor at the university.

To assess the quality of different hypothesis induced from different restrictions we varied the values of parameters *clauselength, evalfn* and *noise* in the workflow execution. In the first case, the parameter values ranged from 5 to 10 as a literal of maximum size induced rules. In the second case, the following optimization functions were considered *cover, mestimate* and *compression*. In the third case, the value of the *noise* parameter ranged from 0 to 100, from 10 in 10. More details concerning these parameters can be found in Aleph manual. All other parameters remained at their default values in all activities. All these parameters and their associated values lead to 198 possible combinations. Thus, in a single execution of the workflow, SciCumulus creates a pipeline for each of the 198 combinations of parameters and executes them in parallel on virtual machines.

The entire workflow was executed 5 times in order to guarantee a 95 % confidence interval. Next, we describe the computing environments used in all workflow executions and results of the experiments. For each execution we created a virtual cluster composed by virtual machines of the same type. The workflow was executed in 2 different types of virtual machines in Amazon Cloud following the types of virtual machines types recommended in the work of Coutinho *et al.* [29] and Jackson *et al.* [30]. Table 1 shows the hardware configuration of the virtual machines used in the experiments.

Table 1. Details about virtual machine types

Virtual machine type	Processor	RAM	Disk
c3.2xlarge	Xeon E5-2680 2.80 GHz	15 GB	160 GB
m3.2xlarge	Xeon E5-2670 2.50 GHz	30 GB	160 GB

To conduct the performance evaluation we deployed the workflow in the Amazon EC2 cloud using SciCumulus workflow system. We varied the amount of VMs from 1 to 8, which allowed us to execute the workflow using from 1 up to 64 virtual cores in each execution. Before describing the performance results, it is important to provide important information about the workflow. Basically, LPFlow4SN reads a set of files that contain the execution parameters, the XML definition of the workflow and the prolog files that implement Aleph. Depending on the values of parameters and the virtual machines used for the execution, one combination of parameters within the workflow may require hours to complete, but for the sake of simplicity and without loss of generality, in this article each combination of parameters finishes in a few minutes. It is also important to mention that Aleph (that is the core application of the workflow) is considered to be CPU-bound, since it has a higher CPU usage than disk usage. Workflow execution time was analyzed by running on each of the 2 aforementioned virtual machine types. We also collected information about the CPU, memory and disk usage. These data were collected using the System Activity Report (SAR) [31]. We analyzed the average rate of blocks read and written per second from/to the disk. We also collected the time percentage in which the virtual cores were: (i) idle, (ii) performing user processes, and (ii) running OS processes.

When we analyze the total execution time of the workflow we can state by ana-lyzing Fig. 3 that there was a reduction of 95.7 % (with the virtual cluster composed by c3.2xlarge virtual machines) and 94.6 % (with the virtual cluster composed by m3.2xlarge virtual machines) in the execution time when using 64 cores compared to the execution time on a single core of each virtual machine type. Although there was a reduction in the execution time, the associated speedup was 23.64 and 25.28 respec-tively when using 64 cores. This reduced speedup has a reason: there is a context switch overhead, since in some occasions there are more threads executing than available cores, which increases the overhead in context switching.

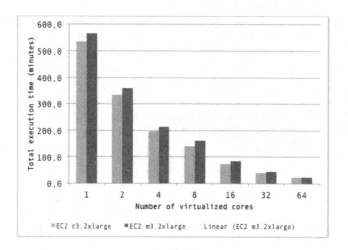

Fig. 3. Execution time of the proposed workflow

We have also measured the percentage of CPU usage during the workflow exe-cution. CPU usage is basically the percentage of time the CPU is actually executing activations *versus* in a wait state. In our experiments, the CPU remains idle when SciCumulus workflow system is scheduling the activities for the several virtual machines. Thus, the percentage of CPU usage for c3.2xlarge and m3.2xlarge are quite similar. In the case of c3.2xlarge we had 91.1 % of CPU usage and in the case of m3.2xlarge we had 90.3 % of CPU usage as presented in Fig. 4.

Likewise the evaluation of total execution time, we also measured the average rate of blocks read and written per second from/to the disk during the workflow execution. These values were respectively 1399.2 and 160.4 for c3.2xlarge and 1265.8 and 141.3 for m3.2xlarge. These results show that the OS present in the virtual machines were able to achieve a relatively efficient access to main memory and disk. These results are acceptable for workflows executed in clouds as stated by Jackson *et al.* [30] (Fig. 5).

The last performed analysis was the financial one. We calculated the financial cost to execute the workflow using these two types of virtual machines when using 64 virtual cores. The financial cost was of US$ 4.20 for c3.2xlarge and US$ 5.60 for

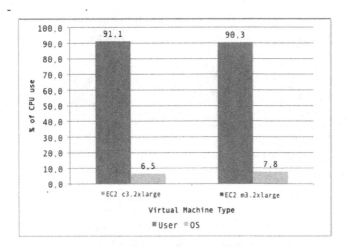

Fig. 4. Percentage of CPU usage

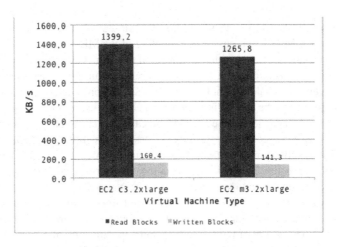

Fig. 5. Disk performance during the workflow execution

m3.2xlarge. It is noteworthy that the costs refer to virtual machines allocated US territory, although Amazon EC2 allows for users to instantiate virtual machines in different countries. The results point out that the c3.2xlarges virtual machines are more cost-effective than m3.2xlarge, because besides having a reduced cost per hour, it was the virtual machine that executed the workflow in the shortest time possible. However, both financial costs are acceptable (Fig. 6).

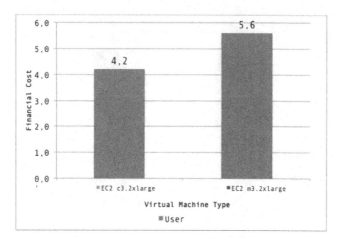

Fig. 6. Financial cost of the workflow execution

5   Conclusions

This paper presented the LPFlow4SN workflow that aims at inferring knowledge in social networks through a MRDM process. The modeling of the MRDM process is performed using ILP techniques associated with the concept of scientific workflow for modeling and structuring process execution. The experiment presented in this paper showed us that social network analysis could benefit from features already provided by existing SWfMS. Because this process can be computing intensive due to the variation of parameter values on a large scale, we chose to use the SWfMS SciCumulus as the basis for LPFlow4SN, since it offers parallel execution capabilities besides the possible *a posteriori* analysis of the results. The results show that there was a reduction of 95.7 % (c3.2xlarge virtual machines) and 94.6 % (m3.2xlarge virtual machines) in the execution time when using 64 cores. Disk access and percentage of CPU usage were also acceptable.

Although we still need various adjustments and improvements in the implementation to reach a generic solution for the analysis of social networks with LPFlow4SN, the results show the benefits of the proposed approach. However, the goal of providing a simple and structured way to run a complex process MRDM process by analysts who are not experts in parallel processing has been met.

Acknowledgments. The authors would like to thank FAPERJ (grant E-26/111.370/2013) and CNPq (grant 478878/2013-3) for partially sponsoring this research.

References

1. Bakshy, E., Rosenn, I., Marlow, C., Adamic, L.: The role of social networks in information diffusion. In: Proceedings of the 21st International Conference on World Wide Web, pp. 519–528, New York, NY, USA (2012)

2. Richardson, M., Domingos, P.: Markov logic networks. Mach. Learn. **62**(1–2), 107–136 (2006)
3. Han, J., Kamber, M., Pei, J.: Data Mining Concepts and Techniques, 3rd edn. Elsevier, Amsterdam (2012)
4. Bloedorn, E., Christiansen, A.D., Hill, W., Skorupka, C., Talbot, L.M., Tivel, J.: Data Mining for Network Intrusion Detection: How to Get Started (2001)
5. Dalal, M.A., Harale, N.D.: A survey on clustering in data mining. In: Proceedings of the International Conference & Workshop on Emerging Trends in Technology, pp. 559–562, New York, NY, USA (2011)
6. Hu, X.: Data mining in bioinformatics: challenges and opportunities. In: Proceeding of the Third International Workshop on Data and Text Mining in Bioinformatics, pp. 1–1, New York, NY, USA (2009)
7. Džeroski, S., Lavrač, N.: Relational Data Mining. Springer, Berlin, New York (2001)
8. Raedt, L.: Logical and relational learning. In: Proceedings of the 19th Brazilian Symposium on Artificial Intelligence: Advances in Artificial Intelligence, pp. 1–1. Springer, Berlin, Heidelberg (2008)
9. Michalski, R.S.: A theory and methodology of inductive learning. Artif. Intell. **20**, 111–161 (1983)
10. Muggleton, S.: Inductive logic programming. In: 6th International Workshop, ILP-96, Stockholm, Sweden, August 1996, Selected Papers. Springer, New York (1997)
11. Nilsson, U., Małuszyński, J.: Logic, Programming, and Prolog. Wiley, Chichester, New York (1995)
12. Mattoso, M., Werner, C., Travassos, G.H., Braganholo, V., Ogasawara, E., Oliveira, D.D., Cruz, S.M.S.D., Martinho, W., Murta, L.: Towards supporting the life cycle of large scale scientific experiments. Int. J. Bus. Process Integr. Manage. **5**(1), 79 (2010)
13. Deelman, E., Gannon, D., Shields, M., Taylor, I.: Workflows and e-Science: an overview of workflow system features and capabilities. Future Gener. Comput. Syst. **25**(5), 528–540 (2009)
14. Taylor, I.J., Deelman, E., Gannon, D.B., Shields, M.: Workflows for e-Science: Scientific Workflows for Grids, 1st edn. Springer, Berlin (2007)
15. Oliveira, D., Baião, F., Mattoso, M.: MiningFlow: adding semantics to text mining workflows. In: First Poster Session of the Brazilian Symposium on Databases, pp. 15–18, João Pessoa, PB, Brazil (2007)
16. Freire, J., Koop, D., Santos, E., Silva, C.T.: Provenance for computational tasks: a survey. Comput. Sci. Eng. **10**, 11–21 (2008)
17. Buneman, P., Khanna, S., Tan, W.-C.: Why and where: a characterization of data provenance. In: Van den Bussche, J., Vianu, V. (eds.) ICDT 2001. LNCS, vol. 1973, pp. 316–330. Springer, Heidelberg (2000)
18. Oliveira, D., Ogasawara, E., Baião, F., Mattoso, M.: "SciCumulus: a lightweight cloud middleware to explore many task computing paradigm in scientific workflows. In: 3rd International Conference on Cloud Computing, pp. 378–385, Washington, DC, USA (2010)
19. de Oliveira, D., Ocaña, K.A.C.S., Baião, F., Mattoso, M.: A provenance-based adaptive scheduling heuristic for parallel scientific workflows in clouds. J. Grid Comput. **10**(3), 521–552 (2012)
20. Oliveira, D., Ogasawara, E., Ocaña, K., Baião, F., Mattoso, M.: An adaptive parallel execution strategy for cloud-based scientific workflows. Concurrency Comput. Pract. Experience **24**(13), 1531–1550 (2012)
21. Alpaydin, E.: Introduction to Machine Learning. MIT Press, Cambridge (2004)
22. Raicu, I., Foster, I.T., Zhao, Y.: Many-task computing for grids and supercomputers. MTAGS **2008**, 1–11 (2008)

23. Wozniak, J.M., Armstrong, T.G., Wilde, M., Katz, D.S., Lusk, E., Foster, I.T.: Swift/T: large-scale application composition via distributed-memory dataflow processing. In: Proceedings of the 13th IEEE/ACM International Symposium on Cluster, Cloud and Grid Computing (CCGrid), pp. 95–102 (2013)

24. Deelman, E., Mehta, G., Singh, G., Su, M.-H., Vahi, K.: Pegasus: mapping large-scale workflows to distributed resources. In: Taylor, I.J., Deelman, E., Gannon, D.B., Shields, M. (eds.) Workflows for e-Science, pp. 376–394. Springer, London (2007)

25. Powers, D.: Evaluation: From Precision, Recall and F-Factor to ROC, Informedness, Markedness & Correlation (2007)

26. Ogasawara, E., Dias, J., Oliveira, D., Porto, F., Valduriez, P., Mattoso, M.: An algebraic approach for data-centric scientific workflows. In: Proceedings of the 37th International Conference on Very Large Data Bases (PVLDB), vol. 4, no. 12, pp. 1328–1339 (2011)

27. Costa, F., Silva, V., de Oliveira, D., Ocaña, K., Ogasawara, E., Dias, J., Mattoso, M.: Capturing and querying workflow runtime provenance with PROV: a practical approach. In: Proceedings of the Joint EDBT/ICDT 2013 Workshops, pp. 282–289, New York, NY, USA (2013)

28. Ailamaki, A.: Managing scientific data: lessons, challenges, and opportunities. In: Proceedings of the 2011 ACM SIGMOD International Conference on Management of Data, pp. 1045–1046. New York, NY, USA (2011)

29. Coutinho, R., Drummond, L., Frota, Y., Oliveira, D., Ocaña, K.: Evaluating grasp-based cloud dimensioning for comparative genomics: a practical approach. In: Proceedings of the Second International Workshop on Parallelism in Bioinformatics, Madrid, Spain (2014)

30. Jackson, K.R., Ramakrishnan, L., Runge, K.J., Thomas, R.C.: Seeking supernovae in the clouds: a performance study. In: Proceedings of the 19th ACM International Symposium on High Performance Distributed Computing, pp. 421–429, New York, NY, USA (2010)

31. Popiolek, P.F., Mendizabal, O.M.: Monitoring and analysis of performance impact in virtualized environments. J. Appl. Comput. Res. 2(2), 75–82 (2013)

32. Liben-Nowell, D., Kleinberg, J.: The link-prediction problem for social networks. J. Am. Soc. Inform. Sci. Technol. 58(7), 1019–1031 (2007)

Methods for Job Scheduling on Computational Grids: Review and Comparison

Edson Flórez[1][(✉)], Carlos J. Barrios[1], and Johnatan E. Pecero[2]

[1] High Performance and Scientific Computing Center - SC3UIS, Universidad
Industrial de Santander, Bucaramanga, Colombia
edson.florez@correo.uis.edu.co, cbarrios@uis.edu.co
[2] Computer Science and Communications Research Unit, University
of Luxembourg, Luxembourg City, Luxembourg
johnatan.pecero@gmail.com

Abstract. This paper provides a review of heuristics and metaheuristics methods, to solve the job scheduling problem in grid systems under the ETC (Expected Time to Compute) model. The problem is an important issue for efficient resource management in computational grids, which is performed by schedulers of these High Performance Computing systems. We present an overview of methods and a comparison of the results reported in the papers that use ETC model. The best methods are identified according to Braun et al. instances [8], which are ETC model instances most used in literature. This survey can help new researchers to lead them directly at the best scheduling algorithms already available to perform deep future works.

Keywords: High performance computing · Grid computing · Combinatorial optimization · Energy efficiency · Heuristics · Scheduling

1 Introduction

High performance computing systems such as grid computing are managed with a Resource Management System (RMS) [5], which typically has a resource manager and a task scheduler to guarantee both quality of service (QoS) provided to users and the requirements of the system administrator [4]. Therefore, an efficient scheduling algorithm is essential to fully exploit grid systems resources [10].

The purpose of this review article is analyze heuristic and metaheuristic approaches to solve job scheduling problem present in grid systems, according to the ETC model, which is a computation model for grid scheduling that allow to formalize, implement and evaluate different scheduling algorithms [20]. For this purpose, the job scheduling context in grid computing is introduced to provide a clear image of the optimization problem tackled, constraints and test cases. Furthermore, the most important heuristic and metaheuristic methods are briefly described.

Then, the analysis focuses on the works that reported their results with the most used ETC model instances, which were proposed by Braun et al. [8], in order to identify the best heuristics accurately. Comparison tables of performance and energy consumption of the reported results are provided. Finally, the outstanding job scheduling algorithms

© Springer International Publishing Switzerland 2015
C. Osthoff et al. (Eds.): CARLA 2015, CCIS 565, pp. 19–33, 2015.
DOI: 10.1007/978-3-319-26928-3_2

are investigated from different points of view, describing the distinctive characteristics of each algorithm, adaptation to the problem, strategies to face the complexity of the problem, etc. However, because a survey of an immense area such as grid scheduling has to focus on certain aspects and neglect others, the scope of the review reported in this article is only the ETC model, therefore, our selection of the best algorithms is only valid in this specific context, the results can be very different with other models and problems.

The paper is organized as follows. Section 2 presents an overview of scheduling problem in grid systems. We have summarized the main heuristics and metaheuristic methods for scheduling in Sect. 3, and we compare and analyze this methods in Sect. 4, delving into the most highlighted. Finally, Sect. 5 presents the main conclusions and lines for future work.

2 Overview of Job Scheduling Problem in Grid Systems

The need of high performance computing in today's society continues to increase and so does the datacenters size and their energy demand, which leads to a rise in the operating costs and carbon emissions. This paper seeks to identify efficient heuristics to allocate independent jobs in the resources of high performance computing systems, with the aiming to minimize energy consumption without affecting the system throughput.

Grid computing infrastructures are typically homogeneous, but the current trend is towards infrastructures with heterogeneous resources, that have nodes with different processing capacity and architectures to run applications or heterogeneous tasks, which gives them a great advantage over homogeneous platforms that deny service to users with different requirements. In heterogeneous infrastructures, job scheduling problem becomes even more complex and essential to the efficient use of resources.

Due to the high complexity of the job scheduling problem (NP-hard [2]) is not possible to determine the optimal solution, because the huge search space cannot be fully explored in reasonable time (polynomial) [18]. This requires approximation methods to find good quality solutions with high computational efficiency instead of algorithms that perform exhaustive searches that require a considerable computing time and resources. Among these are included heuristics and metaheuristic methods of artificial intelligence, such as the Genetic Algorithm (GA) [2].

2.1 Scheduling Problem in Grid Systems

Grid computing infrastructures may be focused on system or users. When is system-centred, the overall performance of the cluster is optimized as disk space, access range and energy consumption, so don't satisfy the users requirements. Instead, when is user-centred, criteria related utility achieved by users are evaluated, such as cost and execution time of their tasks, which can degrade system performance. The balance point (which covers the interests of the user and system administrator) is maximize the resource utilization holding good response times for users requests.

Performance metric most studied in the literature of grid scheduling is the make-span [3, 38], its minimization is a system administrator requirement because it allows to maximize resource usage, while improves the quality of service provided to the user, by reducing of the flowtime or length of the time interval between the release time and completion time of the task [9], which is related to the response times. The makespan is the *maximum completion time* C_i of the tasks [16, 17], is the time when the last task is finished, i.e., the ending time (or length) of the schedule [6]. Moreover, the energy efficiency is a very important issue for system administrator, established as performance per power consumption, to reduce high costs of operating the computing infrastructure, caused by high energy consumption of its multiple processors and the necessity of cooling to dissipate the heat produced.

Types of Job Scheduling. A job is defined as a monolithic application (i.e., a single task) or a collection of tasks, which can be dependent or independent [14]. Tasks are indivisible computational workload units, if they are dependent tasks, have to accomplish a predefined order dependencies between them, and if they are independent tasks, task doesn't require any communication with others [39].

Resources of HPC infrastructures are managed with Resource Management System (RMS), which defines how the computing resources are used to execute the user's tasks, by a dynamic or static scheduling. The dynamic scheduling takes into account the changing resources state, so schedule is modified on-line [11], by adding or removing processors to the jobs. In static scheduling is considered that the resources are available during a time interval (between two successive activations scheduler) and all jobs are known a priori [11], so the schedule is produced off-line, i.e., before starting its execution (and is not modified during execution).

Similarly, job processing can be batch type or immediate [20]; in immediate scheduling or on-line, jobs are assigned individually regardless the tasks that arriving after to the system, without resource planning. Instead, batch scheduling has a compute phase of tasks schedule, where these are grouped into batches, and then at the assign phase, tasks are allocated to selected resources according to the planning of the scheduler [20]. Due to jobs are assigned in groups, each job must wait for the next time interval when the scheduler get activated again. An immediate scheduling algorithm is most appropriate for clusters with low concurrence (which have good availability of resources), i.e., the job arrival rate is small having thus available resources to execute jobs immediately [20], at the time they are submitted by user, without any waiting time in queue. However, batch scheduling can take advantage of job information and compatible resources characteristics, for resource planning where determines which job is most suited to allocate to each resource, thus resulting in better makespan than immediate scheduling [6]. We considered static job scheduling type batch with instances produced under the ETC model [31].

2.2 ETC Computational Model

ETC is a computational model for grid scheduling, with which problem instances are easily represented, helping to the implementation and evaluation of scheduling algorithms. It is based on a normal distribution or gamma to produce ETC matrices that contain estimated processing time of each task in each machine of the system [31].

Formal Definition of the Problem. A computational grid composed by a set of t independent tasks to be assigned and m machines available for planning, with an execution time ETC$[t_i][m_j]$ previously known [2], which represents tasks and machines characteristics such as the computing capacity of machines and the workload of tasks. The workload of real applications can be obtained from specifications provided by the user, historical data or predictions [20].

Objective function: Minimize energy consumption E and makespan $C_{max} = \max\limits_{i \in tarea} (C_i)$

Constrains: Problem is subject to constrains that guarantee that each task is assigned at least once [6], and that each machine only execute a task at a time [19].

Problem Instances. The problem instances are matrices ETC of size txm (t tasks and m machines) [17]. ETC model is characterized by the parameters consistency, machine heterogeneity and task heterogeneity [31]. Table 1 has a high variation along the column that is the high heterogeneity of tasks, and in Table 2, the large variation along a row represents high heterogeneity of machines.

Consistency is defined by the relation between a task and how it is executed in the machines according to heterogeneity of each one [8]. ETC matrix is consistent if a given machine m_j executes any task t_i faster than machine m_k, then machine m_j executes all tasks faster than machine m_k [31], as in Tables 1 and 2. If this occurs only partially, i.e., it has an inconsistent matrix that include a consistent sub-matrix, the matrix is considered semi-consistent. And if it does not have at least consistent submatrices, then it is an inconsistent instance.

Instances are labeled as x_ttmm [17], where x indicates the type of matrix consistency (c for consistent, s for semi-consistent, i for inconsistent), tt indicates the heterogeneity of tasks and mm indicates the heterogeneity of machines. For machines and tasks, "hi" and "lo" mean high and low heterogeneity respectively. With these heterogeneity and consistency features, twelve types of ETC instances are obtained.

Table 1. High heterogeneity of tasks and low heterogeneity of machines in ETC matrix of size 10×5

	m_1	m_2	m_3	m_4	m_5
t_1	11648,23	11803,25	13198,95	14208,43	15309,41
t_2	12826,31	13439,28	13326,27	15145,01	15323,84
t_3	10394,73	10543,99	10629,78	12025,45	14339,22
t_4	508,99	561,11	567,35	766,93	858,48
t_5	5084,65	5288,79	5872,92	6503,83	7001,72
t_6	1808,62	1869,03	1936,83	1987,72	2229,49
t_7	877,99	901,28	956,57	1039,97	1044,57
t_8	5331,69	5858,57	6379,28	6985,41	7339,16
t_9	25250,93	25747,22	25785,37	26322,56	26332,69
t_{10}	3905,32	4012,28	4016,58	4511,21	4521,13

Table 2. Low heterogeneity of tasks and high heterogeneity of machines in ETC matrix of size 10 × 5

	m_1	m_2	m_3	m_4	m_5
t_1	896,03	1033,62	3276,71	16061,46	25993,39
t_2	913,99	1573,82	2928,01	18939,34	27081,67
t_3	802,42	1220,04	2489,74	17588,49	25076,18
t_4	764,43	1389,37	2733,12	17863,56	27848,96
t_5	987,75	1524,07	3622,65	16750,89	24889,36
t_6	658,35	1379,73	2940,43	16916,91	23134,42
t_7	844,28	1437,73	2571,79	14899,55	25771,68
t_8	702,05	1504,82	2955,61	17555,64	25156,15
t_9	642,51	1053,21	3156,67	15995,97	26244,13
t_{10}	866,42	1589,23	2233,13	15738,73	26766,26

The most used instances are twelve ETC matrices of size 512 × 16 proposed by Braun et al. [8], one for each type of ETC instance.

2.3 Energy Model

Energy consumption of the objective function is determined through an energy model, which calculates the energy consumed by each processor in a time interval. Energy consumption by processors is defined as [2]:

$$E = P * \sum_{i=1}^{m} CT_i \qquad (1)$$

Energy consumption depends of processor power P (watts) and how long it is operational CT (Completion Time). Operating system can self-regulate dynamically the supply voltage and clock frequency of the processor with techniques such as DVFS (Dynamic Voltage Frequency Scaling) [7, 13], to save energy and produce less heat. This is represented by discrete values of power, and processor power is adjusted to a minimum power when idle, and switches to the maximum power when processing a task.

In the work of Pinel and Bouvry [7], they proposed a more comprehensive energy model defined in Eq. 2, where BL is a constant power term, N is the number of machines powered on (a machine which is not used is considered powered off) [7], P_{high} y P_{low} is the CPU power consumption when operating at maximum y minimum voltage/frequency respectively.

$$E = BL * N * C_{max} + \sum_{i=1}^{m} (P_{high} * CT_i + P_{low} * (C_{max} - CT_i)) \qquad (2)$$

3 Heuristic and Metaheuristic Methods for Job Scheduling in Grids

3.1 Heuristics of Job Scheduling

Some heuristic algorithms generate solutions from scratch by adding components to a partial solution, step by step, according to a transition rule until a solution is complete. The job scheduling problem present in clusters has been resolved by low complexity heuristics, which consume less time and memory to generate a schedule. A well-known heuristic is Min-Min, which begins with the set of all unmapped tasks, then the minimum expected completion time for each task of the set is establish, and the task with the lowest minimum completion time is selected and assigned to the corresponding machine, next the newly mapped task is removed from the set, and the process repeats until all tasks are mapped [8]. Max-Min works the same way that Min-Min, but according to the maximum expected completion time.

In a recent paper, Diaz et al. [17] compare Min-Min with *low complexity heuristics* Max-Max-Min, Avg-Max-Min and Min-Max-Min in Heterogeneous Computing Systems (HCS), and implemented Task Priority Diagram (TPD) algorithms. TPD defines a graph to set the precedence for each task based on the ETC value, using a Hasse diagram. Regarding makespan metric, *low complexity heuristics* were the best in *inconsistent* and *semi-consistent* scenarios, in consistent scenarios the TPD-based heuristics were better. Díaz et al. [15] compare Min-Min with the algorithms Min-Min-Min, Min-Mean-Min y Min-Max-Min, and were evaluated performance, energy efficiency and scalability in large-scale systems. Among this algorithms family were not presented significant differences in performance metrics (makespan and flowtime) and scalability, however, regarding the energy efficiency Min-Min was highlighted over the others.

Others specialized heuristics for job scheduling problems in distributed systems are Opportunistic Load Balancing (OLB), Minimum Execution Time (MET), Minimum Completion Time (MCT), Sufferage and High Standard Deviation First. In the extensive work of Braun et al. [8], where eleven heuristics are evaluated using the ETC model, a genetic algorithm obtained the lowest makespan, MCT heuristic outperformed to MET, and OLB got the worst makespan. OLB try to keep all machines as busy as possible, assigns each task to the next machine that is expected to be available, however, due to OLB does not consider expected task execution times, can result in a very long makespan [8]. MET try to assigns each task to the machine where is execute faster, i.e., the machine with the best expected execution time for that task, but because regardless of that machine's availability (current workload), this can cause a severe load imbalance across machines. MCT try to assigns each task to the machine with the minimum expected completion time for that task, in this manner seek to avoid the circumstances in which OLB and MET perform poorly [8]. But this causes some tasks to be assigned to machines that do not have the minimum execution time for them.

High Standard Deviation First (MaxStd) assigns first the task with the highest standard deviation of the expected execution time of the task, to the machine that has the minimum completion time, since the delay produced by their allocation will not affect too much the total makespan. This standard deviation represents the amount variation in task execution time on different machines [2].

Sufferage is the difference between the best and the second-best minimum completion time of the task [2, 32]. Task with the highest sufferage is assigned to the task's second most favourable machine, because in other way would be the most delay.

3.2 Metaheuristics of Job Scheduling

HPC literature has more complex techniques known as metaheuristics, approaches that have been used to solve many optimization problems, and could be a basis to design efficient grid schedulers [20]. These find sub-optimal solutions of high quality, with less evaluations of solutions for combinatorial optimization problems, however, usually require long run times [20], much higher than run times of heuristics. The main metaheuristics that have been applied in job scheduling are shown in Table 3, along with their basic characteristics and related works. Some of these works follow the ETC model and most are about job scheduling in grid.

Some metaheuristics have random components, such as mutations in Evolutionary Algorithms, and additional information produced by itself, such as pheromone in Ant Colony Optimization, to guide and diversify the search for solutions. Even so, it cannot guarantee the finding of optimal solution, only can find approximate solutions. These methods depend much of quality and diversity of the initial solution, which is usually generated randomly to ensure diversity. Some methods are multi-boot, to explore other solutions to direct the search towards regions of the search space where the global optima is located, instead of getting stuck in a local optima. Metaheuristics can be based in local search and population.

Table 3. Basic characteristics of metaheuristics [12]

Metaheuristic	Characteristics	References
Simulated annealing	Acceptance criterion	30
	Cooling schedule	
Tabu search	Neighbor choice (tabu list)	29
	Aspiration criterion	
Evolutionary algorithms	Recombination	2, 8, 21, 22, 23, 24
	Mutation	
	Selection	
Ant colony optimization	Probabilistic construction	25, 26, 27
	Pheromone update	
Particle swarm optimization	Population-based	28
	Social coefficient	

Metaheuristics Based in Local Search. A local search heuristic start from some initial solution and iteratively try to replace the current solution by a better solution in an appropriately defined neighborhood of the current solution [12]. Local Search

(LS) is performed until a stopping condition is met, such as a number of consecutive iterations without changing current solution or until the maximum execution time runs out. It only requires a few specifications as an evaluation function and an efficient method for exploring neighbourhood. This deterministic and memoryless method can find solutions quickly, but the final solution strongly depends on the initial solution to avoid getting stuck in the local optima and ensure convergence to suboptimal or optimal solutions.

Tabu Search (TS) in every iteration can accept higher cost solutions to explore other areas of the search space [35], taking into account a tabu list that prevents repeated moves. Xhafa et al. implemented this method under the ETC model [29].

Greedy Randomized Adaptive Search Procedure (GRASP) is a random iterative search method [31], which changes the current solution with a restricted candidate list (RCL) of the best options available, and ends when reach a stopping condition, e.g., achieve a given number of iterations.

Simulated Annealing (SA) is a stochastic search algorithm without any memory [30], inspired by the annealing process in metallurgy. In this process a material (such as steel) is heated to a specific temperature, the heat causes that atoms to increase their energy, and thus can easily move from their initial positions to explore the search space. Then it is gradually cooled until temperature environment, seeking to reach the global optima where material acquires desired physical properties (such as ductility, toughness, etc.). Algorithm starts from a random initial solution and a high probability (initial temperature) to allow any random move, which may be a worst quality solution than current solution, in order to escape the local minima and explore the search space. The probability to accept any movement gradually decrease (cooling) during the search, until become an iterative algorithm that accepts only current solution changes if there is an improvement. Cooling rule may change during the execution of the algorithm, in order to adjust the balance between diversification and intensification of search to converge to a solution [12].

Population-Based Metaheuristics. In population-based metaheuristics, the solution space is explored through a population of individuals. Main metaheuristics in this category are Evolutionary Algorithms, Ant Colony Optimization and Particle Swarm Optimization.

Evolutionary Algorithms (EA) are inspired by the evolution of living beings, so it uses selection and combination mechanisms. The most used of this family algorithms are genetic algorithms (GA), where from an initial population of chromosomes (solution), it seeks to find the most suitable (solution with the best cost in objective function) over the course of several generations, through crossover of chromosomes, random mutations of genes and selection of chromosomes that survive to produce the next generation. Genetic algorithms for the scheduling problem in grid has been quite used, e.g., by Braun et al. [8], Zomaya and Teh [21], Gao et al. [22] and Carretero et al. [23]. Pinel et al. [2] implemented a Genetic Algorithm in a conventional cluster, to which was added millicomputers to reduce power consumption. This algorithm is called PA-CGA (Parallel Asynchronous - Cellular Genetic Algorithm) and was proposed along with a heuristic called 2PH (Two Phase Heuristic), it consists of two phases, Min-Min followed by Local Search. Both algorithms were evaluated against Min-Min, achieving better performance (makespan) with a low runtime. In the work of Nesmachnow et al. [37], proposed the Parallel Micro CHC (Cross generational elitist selection, Heterogeneous recombination and Cataclysmic mutation) algorithm and they obtained an excellent makespan for grid scheduling.

Other evolutionary computation algorithm is the Memetic Algorithm (MA), a hybrid algorithm that combines evolution ideas with local search, through memes (cultural information unit) similar to genes, common information of a population is transmitted to the next generation. Few works have implemented this algorithm for grid scheduling problem because it is a recent algorithm, such as Xhafa et al. [24] that proposes a Cellular MA (cMA) for scheduling under the ETC model.

In the literature several algorithms have been proposed following the Ant Colony Optimization (ACO) probabilistic method, to find approximate solutions to the combinatorial optimization problems as the tackled in our work. The first ACO algorithm was Ant System (AS) proposed by Marco Dorigo, and have been used to solve a similar problem called Job Shop Scheduling [26]. Recent versions gave better results, as the Max-Min Ant System (MMAS) [27]. An implementation of ACO for job scheduling in grid was conducted by Chang et al. [25].

Particle Swarm Optimization (PSO) is similar to ACO algorithm, which seeks to copy the swarming behavior of different living beings (bees, birds, fish, etc.). Abraham et al. proposed an approach for scheduling problem using a fuzzy PSO algorithm [28].

Also have implemented hybrid metaheuristics, mainly with Tabu Search. Other metaheuristic is executed first, e.g., a genetic algorithm that search a good quality solution, and then Tabu Search tries to improve it, exploring the neighborhood of that solution. In works that reported results with the Braun et al. instances [8], have been implemented hybrid metaheuristics MA + TS [34] and ACO + TS [36].

4   Comparison of Scheduling Algorithms

The instances used of Braun et al. benchmark are twelve of 512 jobs and 16 machines, which correspond to the twelve different types of ETC instances. The metrics analyzed in this work are makespan as the indicator of performance, and power consumption to establish energy efficiency according to the achieved performance. Energy efficiency was only determined for algorithms implemented by the Luxembourg University [15, 17], through the execution of algorithms using Braun et al. instances and the energy model (and parameters values) defined by Guzek et al. [40], because only the makespan is reported in most papers reviewed.

4.1   Comparative Analysis

The best makespan obtained for reported algorithms are compared in Table 4, which highlights the evolutionary algorithms Parallel CHC [33] and Parallel Micro CHC [37], the latter achieves the best makespan in all instances. Also it is highlighted Min-Min heuristic [1, 32], as it requires a very low running time to obtain good quality solutions, an issue in which the evolutionary metaheuristics are not very strong. The complete results of all heuristics and metaheuristics are reported in the website http://forge.sc3. uis.edu.co/redmine/documents/1. There you can see that Min-Min is better than all heuristics as Sufferage and Max-Min, and it is known that Min-Min is also better than MET, MCT and OLB heuristics, according to the comparison graphs presented in the work of Braun et al. [8].

Makespan results of Min-Min and Max-Min reported in [32], agree with those obtained in the execution of algorithms provided by the Luxembourg University [15, 17]. Analyzed the makespan for each type of consistency, Min-Min and Sufferage heuristics have a long makespan in consistent and semi-consistent instances, Parallel CHC algorithm is the second best makespan in six of twelve instances, which mostly belong to the type of semi-consistent and inconsistent instances. In the remaining instances is overcome by Tabu Search [35], ACO + TS [36] and PA-CGA [38]. Although the hybrid metaheuristics (ACO + TS and cMA + TS) are not the best in this case, they are a good alternative to be further investigated.

In algorithms that we have the necessary information to assess the multi-objective function, which aims to minimize energy consumption and makespan simultaneously, a score function SF is used [7, 17]. It represents the energy efficiency, also known as fitness function [20], to set the importance of the two objectives with a weight parameter α as follows:

$$SF = \alpha * C_{max} + (1 - \alpha) * E \tag{3}$$

Therefore, the aim will be to minimize the score function. If the priority of both objectives are the same, we can set α at 0.5 to have a balanced weight or importance of makespan and energy. Moreover, it is required to normalize the values of each metric for appropriate calculation of the score (because metrics have different measure units), so the value of makespan and energy obtained by each algorithm is divided by the maximum value of all algorithms [15]. Normalized values are in the range [0,1], where 1 is the worst performance value. The score obtained from the executed algorithms is compared in Fig. 1. Min-Min algorithm is better in all instances with a balanced α at 0.5, and as well with α between 0.1 and 0.9 approximately. Also is outstanding the energy efficiency of Min-Mean-Min and Min-Max-Min. In contrast, Max-Min has one of the worst performance, especially in inconsistent instances where it has the highest energy consumption and makespan.

4.2 Analysis of the Highlighted Algorithms

The highlighted algorithms according to the makespan are Parallel Micro CHC and Parallel CHC algorithms. These evolutionary algorithms have in common its basics characteristics (selection, recombination and mutation), and achieve to find the best solutions for grid scheduling problem, because they have a good balance between random and guided search. Starting from a random initial solution (or obtained with fast heuristics as Min-Min, MCT and Sufferage), explore the search space guided by the information contained in a population of chromosomes. For this is defined a rule to select the fittest individuals, which are recombine to generate new individuals

Table 4. Best makespan of algorithms

Instance 512 × 16	Min-Min [32]	Sufferage [32]	TS [35]	cMA [24]	GA [33]	Parallel GA [33]	PA-CGA [38]	CHC [33]	Parallel CHC [33]	Parallel Micro-CHC [37]	MA + TS [34]	ACO + TS [36]
u_c_hihi.0	8.460.674	10.908.698	7.448.641	7.700.930	7.659.879	7.577.922	7.437.591	7.599.288	7.461.819	**7.381.570**	7.530.020	7.497.201
u_c_hilo.0	161.805	167.483	153.263	155.335	155.092	154.915	154.393	154.947	153.792	**153.105**	153.917	154.235
u_c_lohi.0	275.837	349.746	241.673	251.360	250.512	248.772	242.062	251.194	241.513	**239.260**	245.289	244.097
u_c_lolo.0	5.441	5.650	5.155	5.218	5.239	5.208	5.248	5.226	5.178	**5.148**	5.174	5.178
u_i_hihi.0	3.513.919	3.391.758	2.957.854	3.186.665	3.019.844	2.990.518	3.011.581	3.015.049	2.952.493	**2.938.381**	3.058.475	2.947.754
u_i_hilo.0	80.756	78.828	73.693	75.857	74.143	74.030	74.477	74.241	73.640	**73.378**	75.109	73.776
u_i_lohi.0	120.518	125.689	103.866	110.621	104.688	103.516	104.490	104.546	102.123	**102.051**	105.809	102.446
u_i_lolo.0	2.786	2.674	2.552	2.624	2.577	2.575	2.603	2.577	2.549	**2.541**	2.597	2.554
u_s_hihi.0	5.160.343	5.574.358	4.168.796	4.424.541	4.332.248	4.262.338	4.229.018	4.299.146	4.198.780	**4.103.500**	4.321.015	4.162.548
u_s_hilo.0	104.375	103.401	96.181	98.284	97.630	97.506	97.425	97.888	96.623	**95.787**	97.177	96.762
u_s_lohi.0	140.285	153.094	123.407	130.015	126.438	125.717	125.579	126.238	123.237	**122.083**	127.633	123.922
u_s_lolo.0	3.807	3.728	3.451	3.522	3.510	3.480	3.526	3.492	3.450	**3.434**	3.484	3.455
Average	1.502.545	1.738.759	1.281.544	1.345.414	1.319.317	1.303.875	1.290.666	1.311.153	1.284.600	**1.268.353**	1.310.475	1.284.494

Note: Bold values are the best results

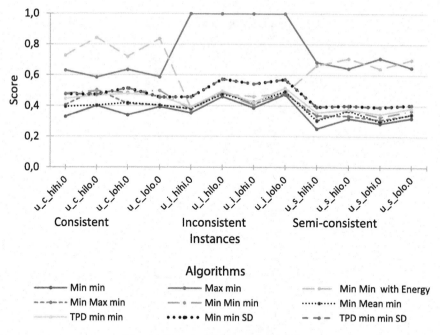

Fig. 1. Energy efficiency of algorithms

(offspring), and with the passing of generations (iterations) it allows to reach a high quality solution. Mutations that occur randomly in traditional evolutionary algorithms, to overcome local optima and diversify the search, in these algorithms are replaced by a mating restriction between very similar individuals and a reset process when the search tends to quickly converge to local optima.

Both algorithms differ mainly in that Parallel Micro CHC includes additional concepts of Micro Genetic Algorithm (μ-GA) [41], to avoid getting stuck in by the lack of diversity in the solutions when small populations are used, through the maintenance of an elite population used to reset the main population each specific number of generations.

Between the heuristics, Min-Min got a good balance between energy consumption and makespan, due to it always first assigns the task to the machine with the overall minimum completion time [8], therefore, the system has more available machines to execute tasks in the best corresponding machine, i.e., the machine with the lowest ETC for the task. Min-Min likely can assign more tasks to their best ETC than Max-Min, which first assigns the tasks to the machine with the maximum completion time. Min-Min heuristic assigns the first task t_i to the machine that finishes it earlier and executes it faster, and for every task assigned after t_i, Min-Min changes the machine availability status by the least possible amount for every assignment. The expectation is that a smaller makespan can be obtained if more tasks are assigned to the machines that complete them the earliest and also execute them the fastest [8].

5   Conclusions and Future Works

This article presented an overview of the most important heuristic and metaheuristic methods to solve the job scheduling problem in grid computing. The algorithms have been compared and analyzed in terms of job scheduling under the ETC model (with the most common instances). In these terms, the evolutionary algorithm Parallel Micro CHC is the best method identified according to the makespan, and full results reported suggest that the evolutionary algorithms are well suited to face the complexity of scheduling problem. The main heuristics are also compared according to the energy efficiency, where the Min-Min algorithm stands out over the other heuristics executed.

With this review article, new researchers can determine the heuristics most prominent nowadays, to implement their diverse search strategies in related combinatorial optimization problems. The main lines for future work include design an evolutionary algorithm of low-complexity to get an appropriated execution time on a low-power computational infrastructure, and minimize both the makespan and energy consumption. The purpose is get a better balance in all types of instances and improve the energy efficiency in HPC resources, so we are working on an ARM-based processors cluster and we will propose an energy model based in experimental data obtained using this platform.

Acknowledgments. The authors thank to the University of Luxembourg for providing us with algorithms to test their performance with instances of Braun et al. benchmark.

References

1. Pinel, F., Pecero, J.E., Khan, S.U., Bouvry, P.: Energy-efficient scheduling on milliclusters with performance constraints. In: Proceedings of the 2011 IEEE/ACM International Conference on Green Computing and Communications, pp. 44–49 (2011)
2. Pinel, F., Dorronsoro, B., Pecero, J.E., Bouvry, P., Khan, S.U.: A two-phase heuristic for the energy-efficient scheduling of independent tasks on computational grids. Cluster Comput. **16** (3), 421–433 (2013)
3. Izakian, H., Abraham, A., Snasel, V.: Comparison of heuristics for scheduling independent tasks on heterogeneous distributed environments. In: International Joint Conference on Computational Sciences and Optimization, vol. 1, pp. 8–12 (2009)
4. He, X., Sun, X., Von Laszewski, G.: QoS guided min-min heuristic for grid task scheduling. J. Comput. Sci. Technol. **18**(4), 442–451 (2003)
5. Iqbal, S., Gupta, R., Lang, Y.: Job scheduling in HPC clusters. Power Solutions, pp. 133–135 (2005)
6. Dutot, P.F., Eyraud, L., Mounié, G., Trystram, D.: Bi-criteria algorithm for scheduling jobs on cluster platforms. In: Proceedings of the Sixteenth Annual ACM Symposium on Parallelism in Algorithms and Architectures, pp. 125–132 (2004)
7. Pinel, F., Bouvry, P.: A model for energy-efficient task mapping on milliclusters. In: Proceedings of the Second International Conference on Parallel, Distributed, Grid and Cloud Computing for Engineering, pp. 1–32 (2011)

8. Braun, T.D., Siegel, H.J., Beck, N., Bölöni, L.L., Maheswaran, M., Reuther, A.I., Freund, R. F.: A comparison of eleven static heuristics for mapping a class of independent tasks onto heterogeneous distributed computing systems. J. Parallel Distrib. Comput. 61(6), 810–837 (2001)

9. Diaz, C.O., Guzek, M., Pecero, J.E., Danoy, G., Bouvry, P., Khan, S.U.: Energy-aware fast scheduling heuristics in heterogeneous computing systems. In: 2011 International Conference on High Performance Computing and Simulation (HPCS), pp. 478–484 (2011)

10. Leung, J.Y. (ed.): Handbook of Scheduling: Algorithms, Models, and Performance Analysis. CRC Press, Boca Raton (2004)

11. Ali, S., Braun, T.D., Siegel, H.J., Maciejewski, A.A., Beck, N., Bölöni, L., Yao, B.: Characterizing resource allocation heuristics for heterogeneous computing systems. Adv. Comput. 63, 91–128 (2005)

12. Blum, C., Roli, A.: Metaheuristics in combinatorial optimization: overview and conceptual comparison. ACM Comput. Surv. (CSUR) 35(3), 268–308 (2003)

13. Valentini, G.L., Lassonde, W., Khan, S.U., Min-Allah, N., Madani, S.A., Li, J., Bouvry, P.: An overview of energy efficiency techniques in cluster computing systems. Cluster Comput. 16(1), 3–15 (2013)

14. Hussain, H., Malik, S.U.R., Hameed, A., Khan, S.U., Bickler, G., Min-Allah, N., Rayes, A.: A survey on resource allocation in high performance distributed computing systems. Parallel Comput. 39(11), 709–736 (2013)

15. Diaz, C.O., Guzek, M., Pecero, J.E., Bouvry, P., Khan, S.U.: Scalable and energy-efficient scheduling techniques for large-scale systems. In: 11th International Conference on Computer and Information Technology (CIT), pp. 641–647 (2011)

16. Barrondo, A., Tchernykh, A., Schaeffer, E., Pecero, J.: Energy efficiency of knowledge-free scheduling in peer-to-peer desktop Grids. In: 2012 International Conference on High Performance Computing and Simulation (HPCS), pp. 105–111 (2012)

17. Diaz, C.O., Pecero, J.E., Bouvry, P.: Scalable, low complexity, and fast greedy scheduling heuristics for highly heterogeneous distributed computing systems. J. Supercomputing 67(3), 837–853 (2014)

18. Dong, F., Akl, S.G.: Scheduling algorithms for grid computing: state of the art and open problems. School of Computing, Queen's University, Kingston, Ontario (2006)

19. Lindberg, P., Leingang, J., Lysaker, D., Bilal, K., Khan, S.U., Bouvry, P., Li, J.: Comparison and analysis of greedy energy-efficient scheduling algorithms for computational grids. In: Energy-Efficient Distributed Computing Systems, pp. 189–214 (2011)

20. Xhafa, F., Abraham, A.: Computational models and heuristic methods for grid scheduling problems. Future Gener. Comput. Syst. 26(4), 608–621 (2010)

21. Zomaya, A.Y., Teh, Y.H.: Observations on using genetic algorithms for dynamic load-balancing. IEEE Trans. Parallel Distrib. Syst. 12(9), 899–911 (2001)

22. Gao, Y., Rong, H., Huang, J.Z.: Adaptive grid job scheduling with genetic algorithms. Future Gener. Comput. Syst. 21(1), 151–161 (2005)

23. Carretero, J., Xhafa, F., Abraham, A.: Genetic algorithm based schedulers for grid computing systems. Int. J. Innovative Comput. Inf. Control 3(6), 1–19 (2007)

24. Xhafa, F., Alba, E., Dorronsoro, B., Duran, B., Abraham, A.: Efficient batch job scheduling in grids using cellular memetic algorithms. In: Metaheuristics for Scheduling in Distributed Computing Environments, pp. 273–299 (2008)

25. Chang, R.S., Chang, J.S., Lin, P.S.: An ant algorithm for balanced job scheduling in grids. Future Gener. Comput. Syst. 25(1), 20–27 (2009)

26. Colorni, A., Dorigo, M., Maniezzo, V., Trubian, M.: Ant system for job-shop scheduling. Belg. J. Oper. Res. Stat. Comput. Sci. 34(1), 39–53 (1994)

27. Stützle, T., Hoos, H.H.: MAX–MIN ant system. Future Gener. Comput. Syst. **16**(8), 889–914 (2000)
28. Liu, H., Abraham, A., Hassanien, A.E.: Scheduling jobs on computational grids using a fuzzy particle swarm optimization algorithm. Future Gener. Comput. Syst. **26**(8), 1336–1343 (2010)
29. Xhafa, F., Carretero, J., Dorronsoro, B., Alba, E.: A tabu search algorithm for scheduling independent jobs in computational grids. Comput. Inform. **28**, 237–250 (2009)
30. Kirkpatrick, S., Vecchi, M.P.: Optimization by simulated annealing. Science **220**(4598), 671–680 (1983)
31. Ali, S., Siegel, H.J., Maheswaran, M., Hensgen, D., Ali, S.: Representing task and machine heterogeneities for heterogeneous computing systems. Tamkang J. Sci. Eng. **3**(3), 195–208 (2000)
32. Xhafa, F., Barolli, L., Durresi, A.: Batch mode scheduling in grid systems. Int. J. Web Grid Serv. **3**(1), 19–37 (2007)
33. Nesmachnow, S., Cancela, H., Alba, E.: Heterogeneous computing scheduling with evolutionary algorithms. Soft. Comput. **15**(4), 685–701 (2010)
34. Xhafa, F.: A hybrid evolutionary heuristic for job scheduling on computational grids. In: Hybrid Evolutionary Algorithms, pp. 269–311 (2007)
35. Xhafa, F., Carretero, J., Alba, E., Dorronsoro, B.: Design and evaluation of tabu search method for job scheduling in distributed environments. In: Proceedings of the 22th International Parallel and Distributed Processing Symposium, pp. 1–8 (2008)
36. Ritchie, G., Levine, J.: A hybrid ant algorithm for scheduling independent jobs in heterogeneous computing environments. In: Proceedings of the 23rd Workshop of the UK Planning and Scheduling Special Interest Group, pp. 178–183 (2004)
37. Nesmachnow, S., Cancela, H., Alba, E.: A parallel micro evolutionary algorithm for heterogeneous computing and grid scheduling. Appl. Soft Comput. **12**(2), 626–639 (2012)
38. Pinel, F., Dorronsoro, B., Bouvry, P.: A new parallel asynchronous cellular genetic algorithm for scheduling in grids. In: 2010 IEEE International Symposium on Parallel Distributed Processing, Workshops and PhD Forum, pp. 1–8 (2010)
39. Bardsiri, A.K., Hashemi, S.M.: A comparative study on seven static mapping heuristics for grid scheduling problem. Int. J. Softw. Eng. Appl. **6**(4), 247–256 (2012)
40. Guzek, M., Pecero, J.E., Dorronsoro, B., Bouvry, P.: Multi-objective evolutionary algorithms for energy-aware scheduling on distributed computing systems. Appl. Soft Comput. **24**, 432–446 (2014)
41. Coello Coello, C.A., Toscano Pulido, G.: A micro-genetic algorithm for multiobjective optimization. In: Zitzler, E., Deb, K., Thiele, L., Coello Coello, C.A., Corne, D.W. (eds.) EMO 2001. LNCS, vol. 1993, pp. 126–140. Springer, Heidelberg (2001)

Cloud Computing for Fluorescence Correlation Spectroscopy Simulations

Lucía Marroig[1], Camila Riverón[1], Sergio Nesmachnow[1],
and Esteban Mocskos[2,3(✉)]

[1] Universidad de la República, Montevideo, Uruguay
{lucia.marroig,camila.riveron,sergion}@fing.edu.uy
[2] Departamento de Computación, Facultad de Ciencias Exactas y Naturales,
Universidad de Buenos Aires, Buenos Aires, Argentina
emocskos@dc.uba.ar
[3] Centro de Simulación Computacional p/Aplic. Tecnológicas/CSC-CONICET,
Godoy Cruz 2390, Buenos Aires C1425FQD, Argentina

Abstract. Fluorescence microscopy techniques and protein labeling set
an inflection point in the way cells are studied. The fluorescence correlation spectroscopy is extremely useful for quantitatively measuring the
movement of molecules in living cells. This article presents the design
and implementation of a system for fluorescence analysis through stochastic simulations using distributed computing techniques over a cloud
infrastructure. A highly scalable architecture, accessible to many users,
is proposed for studying complex cellular biological processes. A MapReduce algorithm that allows the parallel execution of multiple simulations
is developed over a distributed Hadoop cluster using the Microsoft Azure
cloud platform. The experimental analysis shows the correctness of the
implementation developed and its utility as a tool for scientific computing in the cloud.

Keywords: Scientific computing · Cloud · Fluorescence analysis

1 Introduction

Nowadays, cloud computing is a major paradigm for solving complex problems [3,13], providing an easy-to-use and ubiquitous platform to process and
store large volumes of data. In recent years, scientific computing systems have
been steadily moving their applications and data to cloud datacenters that provide a comprehensive number of services, including storage and processing.

In addition, new platforms for developing cloud computing applications have
been introduced. Microsoft Azure [9] is one of the most popular cloud platforms
for building, deploying and managing applications in distributed datacenters.
Azure provides the PaaS and IaaS models for cloud computing [3] and provides support for many programming languages, tools, and frameworks, including those commonly used to build large scientific computing applications.

This project has been partially supported by the *Microsoft Azure for Research
Award*.

This article describes a collaborative and interdisciplinary initiative between institutions in Argentina and Uruguay. The project supports the study of complex processes in early stages of embryonic development, using fluorescence techniques [5]. Due to the growing need to execute complex models and manage large volumes of data within reasonable times, we aim at developing an efficient simulation software that models the complex biological reality, supporting multiple users simultaneously, using cloud computing techniques. The developed system makes use of distributed computing in the Microsoft Azure cloud to host and process the simulation software.

The proposed architecture aims for a highly scalable and adaptable design, taking advantage of the available tools provided by Microsoft Azure, for both, hosting and managing a distributed environment, and processing and retrieving to the final user large amounts of data.

The main contributions of the research reported in this article include: (i) an easy-to-use system, facilitating the usability of a biological software analysis; (ii) a paradigm for separating the execution of the simulation programs from the local environment of each user, by applying distributed computing; and (iii) an innovative architecture and implementation for a scientific application using the novel Microsoft Azure cloud infrastructure.

2 Biological Problem Description

This section presents a description of the problem, techniques, and software tools and a brief review of related work.

2.1 Fluorescence Correlation Spectroscopy

Fluorescence Correlation Spectroscopy (FCS) is a well-known technique applied to obtain quantitative information regarding the motion of molecules in living cells. It is based on the analysis of intensity fluctuations caused by fluorescence-labeled molecules moving through the small detection volume of a confocal or two-photon excitation microscope.

Figure 1 shows a schema of an experiment. Fluorescent tagged molecules diffuse and some of them emit photons when they are under the observation volume defined by the laser beam. The photon emission is a stochastic process, its probability is related to the relative position of the molecule and the beam center, which is the most probable position, while the probability diminishes when moving out (Eq. 1), ω_{xy} and ω_z are the radial and axial waists of the point spread function. Standard values for the parameters are: $\omega_{xy} = 0.2\,\mu m$ and $\omega_z = 1\,\mu m$.

$$g(x, y, z) = \exp\left(\frac{-2(x^2 + y^2)}{\omega_{xy}^2} + \frac{-2z^2}{\omega_z^2}\right) \qquad (1)$$

FCS has been applied to study diffusion, transport, binding, and other processes [5]. In the case of simple scenarios such as molecules passively moving in a homogeneous media, the FCS analysis yields analytic functions that can be fitted to the experimental data to recover the phenomenological parameters (e.g., diffusion coefficients, chemical rate constants, etc.). However, many dynamical processes in cells do not follow these simple models, so it is not possible to obtain an analytic function through the theoretical analysis of a more complex model [5]. In those cases, the experimental analysis can be combined with Monte Carlo simulations to help with the interpretation of the experimental data recovered in FCS experiments (see for example, [8]). The comparison between the expectations for

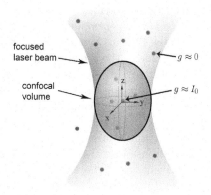

Fig. 1. Schema of a FCS experiment: fluorescent labeled molecules can emit photons under the detection volume. This photons are then detected by the optic system and quantified, obtaining a fluorescent trace of the experiment.

a reduced, simulated model and the experimental data could provide important clues of the dynamical processes hidden in the FCS data. Despite of being useful, most Monte Carlo tools used to simulate FCS experiments are developed as sequential ad-hoc programs designed only for specific scenarios.

2.2   Software Components

At cellular scales, a finite number of molecules interact in complex spaces defined by cell and organelle membranes. In order to simulate stochastic cellular events (movements, interactions, other reactions) with spatial realism at reasonable computational cost, specific numerical techniques should be employed.

This allows experimental analysis to be combined with Monte Carlo simulations to aid in interpretation of the data. FERNET (Fluorescence Emission Recipes and Numerical routines Toolkit) is based on Monte Carlo simulations and the MCell-Blender platform [1]. This tool is designed to treat the reaction-diffusion problem under realistic scenarios.

This method enables to set complex geometries of the simulation space, distribute molecules among different compartments, and define interspecies reactions with selected kinetic constants, diffusion coefficients, and species brightness.

MCell [2,11,12] is used as the simulation engine in FERNET; one of its outputs consists in the position of each molecule in the system every time step. These positions are the input for FERNET, which then generates the fluorescent trace. This data is then compared against the experimental data and can support the validation of the proposed model.

These two components are integrated using MapReduce programming model supported by the Azure service HDInsight.

2.3   Related Work

A number of works have studied the application of cloud computing for developing simulation-based scientific applications. Two of the most relevant and recent approaches are described next.

Jakovits and Srirama [7] studied how to adapt scientific applications to the cloud, providing efficiency and scalability, by applying the MapReduce framework. A four-category classification is proposed for cloud algorithms, according to the adaptability to the model, and the performance of MapReduce is studied for each category. The main results confirm that MapReduce adapts well to embarrassingly parallel applications, but fails to efficiently solve complex models involving a large number of iterations. The authors suggest using the Twister framework for implementing iterative algorithms in the cloud. At a high level of abstraction, this article is helpful to orientate researchers seeking to migrate their applications to the cloud, and the proposed classification is a valuable tool to decide which framework to use according to the research objectives and features.

Richman et al. [10] studied how cloud computing can be used effectively to perform large scientific simulations using the *parameter sweep* paradigm. By executing in parallel, the approach increases the system performance and allows solving complex problems in reasonable execution times. As a relevant case-of-study, the authors describes the implementation of an application to evaluate the life-cycle energy for 1.080.000 scenarios of houses' design in Toronto, over the Amazon Web Services, Simple Storage Service using 24 virtual machines. The proposed implementation reduced the execution times from 563 days to 28 days, by using a uniform data decomposition in blocks that demands almost the same time to be processed. The results show that an appropriate cloud architecture is able to provide significant reductions in the execution time of simulation-based scientific applications, allowing to perform exhaustive parameterization analysis.

On the other hand, our research group has been working on the application of distributed computing techniques (i.e., grid and cloud) applied to scientific computing. Garcia et al. [6] applied the distributed computing paradigm for developing and executing scientific computing applications in the GISELA grid infrastructure, a previous version of nowadays user-oriented grid/cloud systems. Two applications were migrated, both involving the distributed execution of simulations, regarding image processing and computational fluid dynamics, respectively. The study allow us to conclude that efficient processing is a viable option for scientific applications by using the distributed computing paradigm, especially when using the parameter sweep approach and scientific simulations.

In Da Silva et al. [4], we studied the first proposal of applying distributed computing to the simulation of biological processes. MCell and FERNET software packages were executed over a volunteer grid/cloud system, using heterogeneous computing resources from universities in Argentina, Brazil, Mexico, and

Uruguay. A domain decomposition approach was applied to distribute the simulations for six problem models, and the results demonstrated that distributing computing allows performing a large number of simulations in significantly lower execution times than the ones required by a sequential approach.

In this work, we propose an extension to design and implement a fully cloud version of a distributed biological application for applying the FCS technique to study the embryonic development. The application is developed and deployed over a cloud infrastructure, the Microsoft Azure framework.

3   System Architecture for the Cloud

This section describes the architecture of the proposed distributed application for FCS simulations.

3.1   Architecture Design and Application Flow

Most scientific applications can be described as *batch* processes, usually involving a high CPU and RAM utilization, with very low or even no user intervention. Both software components we propose to adapt to a cloud environment, MCell and FERNET, are batch applications with standard features, like reading an initial file, applying a file processing, and finally post-processing to obtain output files that store the results. MCell and FERNET can be run in parallel independently, thus the problem is classified as *embarrassingly parallel*, requiring almost no synchronization between parallel tasks to obtain the final results.

One of the input parameters for a MCell simulation is the definition of reactions, i.e. how molecules act as they approach to each other. Each reaction has an occurrence probability (*rate*). The *rate* parameter might not be known beforehand, so it is interesting to provide the user the ability to define a range of values and the step to go from the lower to the higher value for the *rate* parameter using a parameter sweep application.

Taking into account the features of both MCell and FERNET, we propose designing the distributed system for allowing the user to execute independent simulations and to obtain the results at any time. The architecture seeks to use the elastic capabilities of the Microsoft Azure cloud for executing a large number of instances of MCell-FERNET in parallel, and performing more efficient simulations than in a local execution environment.

The flow of the distributed application is described as follows:

1. Users access the system using a web portal. They configure the scenario to execute MCell/FERNET (some parameters admit a range of values that generate multiple simulations). The system returns a job identification (`jobID`), allowing the users to monitor tasks and get results.
2. A *worker role* is used to obtain the parameters and create the input files for the different simulations. This role also stores the parameter values in order to make them public and accessible to the other roles.

3. Another *worker role* takes the input files to configure and run the simulations in parallel by using the MapReduce paradigm in a HDInsight cluster. This role monitors and stores metadata about the status of running tasks to provide information to the users during the process.
4. The HDInsight cluster implements and executes multiple simulations. It creates compressed files that contains the outputs of FERNET that can be retrieved later by the users.
5. Users can access the website at any time, check the tasks' status by using the jobID, and finally get the resulting files from several executions.

Figure 2 describes the main components of the proposed architecture and the user interaction with the runtime environment to match the described application flow. Users access through a friendly interface to set up the simulation via the *Web role*. The parameter information is then sent from the web role to the *Message Processing* worker role, via a service exposed by this role to send asynchronous messages, using the *Windows Communication Foundation* (WCF) platform. After receiving the message, the *Message Processing* worker role creates the input files for the simulations to run in parallel, and stores them in the storage account, creating *blobs* for each of them using a RESTful service. After that, the role calls a WCF service exposed by the Job Creation worker role, which creates the tasks that are executed on the HDInsight cluster. *Job Creation* also monitors the execution of each task, by storing the state of the tasks for future references. Furthermore, the results and control files generated by tasks that runs on the HDInsight cluster are also stored under the *blob* structure.

Users may request information about the simulations status using the jobID at any time. In this way, the website controls the files created by the worker role Job Creation, and presents this information in a user friendly interface.

3.2   Storage

Storage is the central component of the architecture. All other components communicate with the storage repository at some point in the flow.

An *Azure Storage Account* using the *blob* storage format is used. The access to the storage account is needed for reading, creating, and deleting data. It is performed by using RESTful services, providing an efficient communication and allowing the storage component to work without the need of maintaining states.

We use the geo-redundant capabilities of the Azure storage system to mitigate the effect of the storage element as a potential single point of failure for the proposed system. The system keeps copies of the data in six different geographically distant locations, three of them with at least a distance of 600 km., therefore the probability that all the storage instances fail simultaneously is almost null.

3.3   Fault Tolerance

Fault tolerance is provided automatically by the Azure platform.

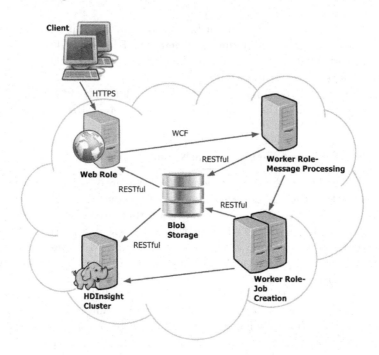

Fig. 2. Diagram of the proposed system architecture over the cloud

The use of page blobs guarantees that each blob is triple-replicated within the datacenter itself, then geo-replicated to a neighboring datacenter. The SLA for storage guarantees 99.9 % availability. Regarding communications (message passing), the use of WCF provides reliable messaging using queues and a send-retry mechanism. The MapReduce engine in HDinsight has an automatic method for retrying the execution of failed tasks. Finally, the cloud service itself is of PaaS type, so the underlying computing infrastructure is completely handled by the service provider according to the High Availability SLA in Azure (availability > 99 % for each role having two or more instances).

4   Implementation Details

This section provides the main implementation details of the system components.

4.1   Web Role

The *web role* is the user access point to the application. It has a running instance of Internet Information Services (IIS), allowing the role to host the project website. A *backend* is provided to access the blob storage and communicate with other roles by using WCF. The web role needs to access the storage because it is in charge of assigning the jobID to each submission, to allow the users to monitor the status of their tasks and retrieve the results of the simulations.

Web roles support a wide number of customers due to horizontal scaling provided by Azure. The Azure service contract specifies that for all Internet oriented virtual machines that has two or more deployed instances on the same availability zone, an external connectivity of at least 99.9 % of the time is granted.

4.2   Message Processing Worker Role

Message processing is implemented by a worker role that reads the user input and performs a parametric sweep on the parameters to create the input files for executing MCell/FERNET. Message Processing exposes a service through a WCF access point, to receive messages sent by the web role. When a message from the web role arrives, the input files are created, information is stored, and an access point exposed by the *Job Creation* role is called using WCF. Since WCF ensures that each message reaches its recipient, after sending the message the role returns to idle state awaiting further calls from the web role.

A parameter sweep algorithm generates different combinations of parameter values to run parallel simulations in the HDInsight cluster. It is defined by: (i) $\mathbf{v}$: the resulting vector of applying a function to the parameters. For the current implementation, $\mathbf{v}$ is the result of executing MCell using some parameters combination; (ii) n: the number of parameters over which the parametric sweep is applied; (iii) $\mathbf{p}$: the vector with the n parameter values that produce results in $\mathbf{v}$. In the current implementation, it corresponds to the specification for the different *rate* values for each reaction, generating the result $\mathbf{v}$ from running MCell; (iv) $\mathbf{j}$: vector of indexes indicating the values for each of the n parameters, within a set of parameter values; (v) $\mathbf{P}$: a $m \times n$ matrix of possible parameter values, being m the number of possible values for each index j; (vi) $\mathbf{L}$: a Boolean vector indicating when using a full or selective parametric sweep, according to $L_k \neq j_k, \forall k = 0, (n-1)$, then the full parametric sweep is applied, otherwise, the partial one is applied.

Algorithm 1 describes the parameter sweep. The *inival* and *endval* vectors are used to define the $\mathbf{P}$ matrix. After setting the parameters, a MDL file is created for each parameter combination using threads, since all files are independent from each other. Each thread creates the MDL file and sends a message to the Job Creation worker role for executing the simulations in the HDInsight cluster.

4.3   Job Creation Worker Role

The implementation of Job Creation is similar to Message Processing, but includes the logic to read the MDL file and configures a MapReduce job to be executed in the HDInsight cluster. The main reason for decoupling Job Creation and Message Processing is that the former performs task monitoring and update status to allow task tracking by the users. If Message Processing and Job Creation were combined in a single worker role, it will use resources continuously, generating a bottleneck when many users execute jobs in the system at the same time. The impact of the bottleneck is reduced by separating the roles: (i) Message Processing is available to receive new messages from the users, processing

Algorithm 1. Parametric sweep algorithm

```
 1: initialize vectors of initial and final values for each reaction (inival, endval)
 2: initialize vector of steps for each reaction (steps)
 3: define the Boolean vector L
 4: j ← [n]
 5: for k = 0 to n − 1 do
 6:     if k = L[k] then
 7:         inival[k] ← inival[k] + steps[k]
 8:     end if
 9:     j[k] = inival[k]
10: end for
11: subid = 1
12: z = n − 1
13: while z >= 0 do
14:     if (j[z] − endval[z]) × steps[z] > 0 then
15:         j[z] = inival[z]
16:         z = z − 1
17:     else
18:         NewThread(CreateMDL(subid, parameters))
19:         z = n − 1
20:         subid = subid + 1
21:     end if
22:     if z >= 0 then
23:         j[z] = j[z] + steps[z] +
24:         if z = L[z] then
25:             j[z] = j[z] + steps[z]
26:         end if
27:     end if
28: end while
```

them automatically and improving the user experience, and (*ii*) the availability of Job Creation is supported on the horizontal auto-scaling features of *Cloud Services* from Azure, thus a lower overhead is produced when crating job new instances in the HDInsight cluster.

4.4 HDInsight Cluster

HDInsight is the implementation of Apache Hadoop in Azure. The Hadoop Distributed File System (HDFS) is mapped to a container in a blob storage in Azure. The cluster is formed by a master node and several slave nodes that execute MapReduce tasks and store metadata and results in the blob storage. HDInsight executes in a set of Azure virtual machines, provisioned when the cluster is created, and using Azure SQL Database for storing metadata. The HDInsight Cluster is isolated of the other Azure components, and it is accessed through a secure *gateway* that exposes a single *endpoint* and performs authentication for each component that access the cluster.

4.5 MapReduce

The MapReduce algorithm is organized as follows.

The **Main** class generates and launches the *mapper* and *reducer* tasks required. It performs some YARN configurations and uploads the required files to the distributed cache of Hadoop, providing an efficient way to share data (each file is copied only once per task, using the cache to avoid local copies to hard drives). The required files for a simulation are the MCell and FERNET executables and configuration files, and the required dynamic libraries for execution. The InputFormat class in Hadoop is used to split the input data for the different MapReduce tasks to execute. A chain of two mappers is launched for each MCell+FERNET execution, each one implementing the execution of the corresponding software package for a single simulation.

The `MCell mapper` implements the MCell execution for each simulation submitted by the users. The class `McellMapper.java` extends the `mapper` class in Hadoop, overriding the `map` method. `McellMapper.java` receives (from Job Creation) a key matching the `jobID`, the execution mode for FERNET (*point* for a single execution or *multi* for multiple executions), and the MDL file required for the MCell execution (locally stored with the name `inputMCell.mdl` on the slave node executing the *map* task, and used by the MCell executable, already loaded in the memory of the node, to launch the execution of the simulation). The standard output of the execution is stored in a file with type *out* in a *blob* on the storage account, including the `jobID` and a reference to the owner (user that submitted the job). The data returned by the `MCell mapper` (key and name of the result file) is used for the execution of the correspondent `FERNET mapper`.

The `FERNET mapper` executes FERNET application. It is implemented in the class `FernetMapper.java`, extending `mapper` and overriding the `map` method. The input parameters are the key and name of the output file of the previous MCell execution, stored in a blob in the main storage account. The FERNET configuration file, stored in the Hadoop distributed cache, is also used. The mapper output is a list of pairs $<key,value>$, with the same key, and value is a structure defined in `FernetOutput.java` that specifies the `jobID`, and the name and content of the FERNET output file. Multiple pairs, thus multiple output files, are returned for the *multi* execution mode, and only one file is returned for the *point* mode.

The *Reducer* groups all values with the same key and applies post-processes the results. It is implemented on the `ResultReducer.java` class, which extends the `reducer` class in Hadoop, overriding the `reduce` method. `ResultReducer` receives the `jobID` and all the associated $<key,value>$ pairs. The post-processing is related to analyze the results for parameter sweep applications, applying statistical analysis and generating correlation graphics. A zip file containing the simulation results and the post-processing results is stored in a blob, inside the container of the storage account associated to the HDInsight cluster.

An example of execution flow for a simulation is shown in Fig. 3.

4.6   Load Balancer

Different simulations have different execution times, so a dynamic load balancer was implemented to improve the system performance.

For each instance of each role, the resource utilization (CPU and RAM) is evaluated to determine the instance load. Network traffic is not evaluated because all cluster nodes are within the same network. A specific module was

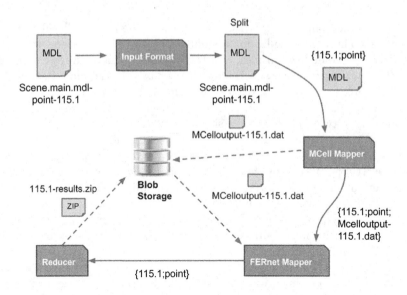

Fig. 3. MapReduce algorithm specification

designed for resource monitoring. We use the `Diagnostics` component in Azure to gather the relevant metrics, and for each resource, the moving average (MA) is computed, considering 10 time periods (in our case, minutes) in the past, for each metric m and instance n: $MA(m,n) = \sum_{i=1}^{i=n} m_i/t$, $t = 10$.

The MAs are used to decide the instance to assign each submission. Instances are classified in four categories according to their loads: *idle*, *low*, *normal*, and *high*. Two thresholds are defined for the CPU load to avoid continuous changes of category: the upper threshold $T_U = 1.3 \times \sum_{i=1}^{i=n} MA(m,i)/n$, (an instance load is 'high' when it is 30 % more loaded than the average load) and lower threshold $T_L = 0.7 \times \sum_{i=1}^{i=n} MA(m,i)/n$ (an instance load is 'low' when it is 30 % less loaded than the average load). According to these values, instances are categorized as: (*i*) *idle* when $MA(CPU,n) < 30\%$; (*ii*) *low* when $30\% < MA(CPU,n) < T_L$ and $MA(mem) < 85\%$; (*iii*) *normal* when $T_L < MA(CPU,n) < T_U$ and $MA(mem) < 85\%$; (*iv*) *high* when $MA(CPU,n) > T_U$ or $MA(mem) \geq 85\%$.

Instances are then selected according to the load characterization. An idle instance is selected for an incoming job if available; otherwise, a low load instance is selected, or in the worst case, a normal one will be selected. Since the load balancer is designed taking into account the metrics that are used for the auto-scaling of the cloud infrastructure, Azure guarantees that there will be at least one instance that is not in the 'high' load category.

5   Validation and Analysis

This section describes the validation and performance analysis of the system.

5.1 Load Balancing

The load balancing technique was evaluated by running 45 simulations arriving at different submission times over the Azure platform (m1.medium instances, dual core virtual machines at 2.0 GHz, 3.75 GB RAM). We worked with a workload involving several simulation bursts, designed to overload the Job Creation worker role. Using the available computing resources, the load balancing algorithm performed well to handle the incoming workloads. Neither of the virtual resources was significantly loaded. In fact, no machine was ever in the 'high load' category, the memory utilization was far below the threshold, while the CPU utilization was between 50 % and 56 % for all machines.

The total time demanded by the load balancer execution was between 572 and 998 ms, showing that no significant overhead is produced by the proposed load balancer when taking into account the large execution times of the simulations.

Table 1. Reactions in the scenario for evaluating parameter sweep applications

Reaction	Initial rate	Final rate	Step
$A + B \rightarrow A$	1.1×10^{-6}	1.2×10^{-6}	0.1×10^{-6}
$B + B \rightarrow A$	0.3	0.4	0.1
$A + A \rightarrow B$	0.06	0.08	0.01

5.2 Parameter Sweep Simulations

The parameter sweep algorithm was tested using a scenario considering three reactions, according to the details presented in Table 1.

The analysis of the execution times for the parameter sweep simulations, reported in Table 2, indicates that the number of possible configurations notably impacts on the execution times, and that no significant differences are shown regarding the number of reactions. In addition, the results also demonstrate that there is a very low overhead for executing a large number of simulations.

Table 2. Execution times for the parameter sweep experiments (s)

# reactions	# combinations				
	4	9	90	200	10000
2	102	120	720	14400	49380
6	–	72	660	12000	62400
10	–	–	660	1020	61200
20	–	–	–	1020	57000

5.3   Fault Tolerance Analysis

Four scenarios were tested to guarantee the proper handling of exceptions due to failures in the application components.

Failure in Message Processing Role. We studied situations when unexpected errors cause Message Processing to shut down, thus forcing the virtual machines for both role instances to restart. This scenario is very unlikely due to the high availability provided by the Azure SLA, but we checked that the system is able to handle this kind of errors. When Message Processing is down and users submit simulations to the web role, an error message appears while the virtual machine are starting, because no agent is active to attend the requests. However, this situation only holds for a few seconds; the system continues operating correctly once the virtual machines for the Message Processing role are up. The whole system recovers successfully and the impact for the user is very limited.

Failure in Job Creation Role. When an unexpected error affect the Job Creation role, the fault tolerance capabilities of WCF guarantees that no messages from Message Processing are lost. Tasks are then launched automatically after Job Creation restarts and the user can access the results without any impact on usability. Again, restarting the role only demands a few seconds.

A different situation happens when the Job Creation role dies when checking and/or updating the status of a given task upon a user request. In that case, the metadata is never updated after the Job Creation restarts, and the user cannot check for the finalization of their job correctly. Thus, an upgraded mechanism was implemented to deal with this issue: task finalization is not only checked by the metadata, but also for the generation of output files for the MapReduce processing. Using this improved implementation, the system provides a transparent, fault tolerant operation regarding the Job Creation role failures.

Failure in MapReduce Task. For testing the tolerance to MapReduce failures, we applied a fault injection strategy. We studied two cases: (*i*) temporary failures in the map or reduce tasks, and (*ii*) failure in the execution due to bad data (i.e., using reactions with some undefined parameter values). In the first case, the inherent capabilities of the HDinsight service allow a correct operation by re-executing the failed tasks. In the second case, the system correctly marked the task as *'failed'* after all attempts were performed, and the user cannot download any MDL files, since no output was generated by the mappers.

5.4   Autoscaling

We also evaluated the auto-scale capabilities of the system deployed in the Azure cloud. We initially launched Message Processing and Job Creation in A1 virtual machines (one core, 2.1 GHz, 1.75 GB RAM), the smallest size recommended for production workloads. Using this basic infrastructure, the roles have not enough resources to deal with multiple users requests, and Azure launches new instances for each role when reaching the default maximum CPU utilization.

When deploying the system on A3 virtual machines (four cores, 2.1 GHz, 7 GB RAM), the CPU utilization of the Message Processing and Job Creation roles is below 25 % in idle state and around 50 % when processing users requests. Thus, we decided to work using two instances for each role, on A3 virtual machines. We modified the Azure auto-scale properties to assure that these two instances are always running, to provide the required 99 % SLA to the system users.

The correct auto-scale behavior of the system was checked by observing the CPU use metric (via *Diagnostics*) and the Azure administration portal.

5.5 Experimental Evaluation of a Realistic Simulation

We used a test case involving one million MCell iterations (see details in Table 3) to test the capabilities of the proposed system when executing large simulations.

Table 3. Input parameters for the realistic simulation

Parameter	Value
ITERATIONS, TIME_STEP	1×10^6, 1×10^{-5}
COORDINATES	$[-1.5, -1.5, -1.5] - [1.5, 1.5, 1.5]$
MOLECULES (*diffusion constant*)	A (5.5×10^{-7}), B (3×10^{-7})
REACTIONS	No reactions
NAME_LIST	A B

A large volume of data (MCell output file: 10 GB) is generated using the previous configuration. By executing this large test, we verified that the simple approach that sends the output of the first mapper to the second one fails due to memory size exception. Thus, we modified the system, implementing a correct strategy to deal with large volumes of data: the output file is stored in a container associated to the HDInsight cluster. This way, all tasks in a MapReduce job can locally access to the file, reading from a buffer and copying the content to the blob, avoiding using a large amount of memory, but a reference to the blob.

The average execution time (over five independent executions) for this large simulation was 5 h and 25 min. There is an overhead due to the data reading, but when using several resources the impact of this overhead is reduced. A parallel analysis considering 10 realistic simulations in the cloud allows achieving almost linear speedup when compared against a sequential execution.

These results confirm that the proposed implementation is a viable option for execution, allowing the users to perform their simulations in the cloud and freeing their local computing resources. The designed architecture and web portal are useful tool for researchers, and the parallel capabilities of the cloud infrastructure allows executing efficiently large simulations.

6   Conclusions

This article presents the design and implementation of a system for fluorescence analysis simulations using distributed computing in a cloud infrastructure.

A highly scalable architecture is proposed for studying complex cellular biological processes, and a MapReduce algorithm for the execution of multiple simulations is developed over a distributed Hadoop cluster using the Microsoft Azure cloud platform. Specific algorithms, including a dynamic load balancer and an application for parametric sweep experiments are also implemented.

Our preliminary experimental evaluation is focused on validating the proposed architecture and the implementation decisions, and testing the capabilities of both the platform and the proposed solution to deal with realistic scenarios for fluorescence analysis simulations.

We obtained promising results, showing that it is possible to adapt scientific systems, such as biological simulations, to a distributed cloud architecture by applying a parallel computing approach using the MapReduce programming model.

The main lines for future work are related to improve the experimental evaluation of the proposed system, especially when considering large simulations and high user demands. In addition, we are working on extending the proposed approach to other biological and scientific computing problems.

References

1. Angiolini, J., Plachta, N., Mocskos, E., Levi, V.: Exploring the dynamics of cell processes through simulations of fluorescence microscopy experiments. Biophys. J. **108**, 2613–2618 (2015)
2. Bartol, T., Land, B., Salpeter, E., Salpeter, M.: Monte carlo simulation of miniature endplate current generation in the vertebrate neuromuscular junction. Biophys. J. **59**(6), 1290–1307 (1991)
3. Buyya, R., Broberg, J., Goscinski, A.: Cloud Computing: Principles and Paradigms. Wiley, New York (2011)
4. Da Silva, M., Nesmachnow, S., Geier, M., Mocskos, E., Angiolini, J., Levi, V., Cristobal, A.: Efficient fluorescence microscopy analysis over a volunteer grid/cloud infrastructure. In: Hernández, G., Barrios Hernández, C.J., Díaz, G., García Garino, C., Nesmachnow, S., Pérez-Acle, T., Storti, M., Vázquez, M. (eds.) CARLA 2014. CCIS, vol. 485, pp. 113–127. Springer, Heidelberg (2014)
5. Elson, E.L.: Fluorescence correlation spectroscopy: past, present, future. Biophys. J. **101**(12), 2855–2870 (2011)
6. García, S., Iturriaga, S., Nesmachnow, S.: Scientific computing in the Latin America-Europe GISELA grid infrastructure. In: Proceedings of the 4th High Performance Computing Latin America Symposium, pp. 48–62 (2011)
7. Jakovits, P., Srirama, S.: Adapting scientific applications to cloud by using distributed computing frameworks. In: IEEE International Symposium on Cluster Computing and the Grid, pp. 164–167 (2013)
8. Kerr, R., Bartol, T., Kaminsky, B., Dittrich, M., Chang, J., Baden, S., Sejnowski, T., Stiles, J.: Fast Monte Carlo simulation methods for biological reaction-diffusion systems in solution and on surfaces. SIAM J. Sci. Comput. **30**(6), 3126–3149 (2008)

 9. Li, H.: Introducing Windows Azure. Apress, Berkely (2009)
10. Richman, R., Zirnhelt, H., Fix, S.: Large-scale building simulation using cloud computing for estimating lifecycle energy consumption. Can. J. Civ. Eng. **41**, 252–262 (2014)
11. Stiles, J.R., Bartol, T.M.: Monte Carlo methods for simulating realistic synaptic microphysiology using MCell, Chap. 4, pp. 87–127. CRC Press (2001)
12. Stiles, J.R., Van Helden, D., Bartol, T.M., Salpeter, E.E., Salpeter, M.M.: Miniature endplate current rise times less than 100 microseconds from improved dual recordings can be modeled with passive acetylcholine diffusion from a synaptic vesicle. Proc. Natl. Acad. Sci. USA **93**(12), 5747–5752 (1996)
13. Velte, T., Velte, A., Elsenpeter, R.: Cloud Computing, A Practical Approach. McGraw-Hill Education, New York (2009)

Porting a Numerical Atmospheric Model to a Cloud Service

Emmanuell D. Carreño$^{(\boxtimes)}$, Eduardo Roloff, and Philippe O.A. Navaux

Informatics Institute - Federal University of Rio Grande Do Sul,
Porto Alegre, Brazil
{edcarreno,eroloff,navaux}@inf.ufrgs.br

Abstract. Cloud Computing emerged as a viable environment to perform scientific computation. The charging model and the elastic capability to allocate machines as needed are attractive for applications that execute traditionally in clusters or supercomputers. This paper presents our experiences of porting and executing a weather prediction application to the an IaaS cloud. We compared the execution of this application in our local cluster against the execution in the IaaS provider. Our results show that processing and networking in the cloud create a limiting factor compared to a physical cluster. Otherwise to store input and output data in the cloud presents a potential option to share results and to build a test-bed for a weather research platform on the cloud. Performance results show that a cloud infrastructure can be used as a viable alternative for HPC applications.

Keywords: Cloud computing · High-performance computing · Numerical atmospheric model

1 Introduction

High performance computing requires a large number of processors interconnected and large data storage. This large-scale scientific computing has been performed per years in costly machines that are out of the possibilities of many research groups. A more common computing infrastructure for HPC is the grid, but this infrastructure is difficult to setup and maintain. Most of the time this work is delegated to PhD students who want to concentrate on their own research rather than setup and manage computing systems [1].

The cloud computing paradigm has provided an alternative to access large infrastructures and resources. In the cloud, the possibility of paying only for the amount of resources used brings convenience for academia. The pay-as-you-go concept could be transformed into a viable option for an institution lacking computing resources.

Request for funding of cloud storage resources may become increasingly common on grant proposals, rather than contributions to capital spending on hardware [2]. But it is clear that one of the major concerns for the HPC community is performance. Some HPC initiatives have started utilizing the cloud for

© Springer International Publishing Switzerland 2015
C. Osthoff et al. (Eds.): CARLA 2015, CCIS 565, pp. 50–61, 2015.
DOI: 10.1007/978-3-319-26928-3_4

their research, but performance concerns of HPC applications in the cloud are immense [3].

Previous work in this area looks only at small HPC benchmarks, which are simple to port or run in most cases. We look at a full and complex HPC application, with difficult requirements as most of the software used in HPC has been optimized to run on specific architectures and require a set of conditions to run in a proper and efficient way. A current problem with those legacy applications is the need to be ported to new infrastructures. The usage of virtualization may solve some of the challenges. In one of our previous work [4], we studied that the cost-efficiency of use cloud computing instead of a cluster is feasible and due to these results we conducted this research.

The goal of this paper is to port a numerical weather prediction application to an IaaS cloud provider and conduct a performance evaluation comparing it to a cluster of physical machines. The main contributions of this paper are the porting process of a legacy application to a cloud provider. Secondly, we created a workflow explaining the steps to execute weather simulations in the cloud provider.

2   Related Work

Langmead et al. [5] executed a DNA sequencing algorithm in Amazon EC2, their work focused on executing a Hadoop application analyzing the costs and the scalability of the application. They conclude that by taking advantage of cloud computing services, it is possible to condense thousand of computing hours into a few hours without owning a cluster.

The use of Amazon EC2 to run an atmosphere-ocean climate model were explored by Evangelinos et al. [6]. In their experiments the performance in the cloud was below the level of a supercomputer, but comparable to a low-cost cluster system. As their major concern was related to latency and bandwidths, they conclude that the usage of Myrinet or Infiniband for the interconnections could help reduce this performance gap.

Johnston et al. [7] implemented a satellite propagation and collision system in Microsoft Azure. They developed an architecture to provide burst capability to their algorithm. The conclusion was that there is potential for cloud-based architectures to deliver cost-effective solutions and confront large-scale problems in science, engineering and business.

The usage of a BLAST algorithm was performed by Lu et al. [8]. They conducted a case study of running data intensive research in the cloud. Their conclusions are that the applications that are compute and data intensive can be executed in the cloud. Additionally they explained that while performance is often considered desirable, scalability and reliability are usually more important for some types of scientific applications.

Simalago et al. [9] performed a study on using cloud to process large data sets. Their experiments with Hadoop conclude that cloud environments could provide some benefits like better resource utilization.

3   Brazilian Regional Atmospheric Modeling System (BRAMS)

In this section, we present the characteristics of the numeric weather prediction application. One of the most widely employed numerical models in the regional weather centers in Brazil is BRAMS [10], a mesoscale model based on RAMS [11]. RAMS, developed by the Atmospheric Science Department at the Colorado State University, is a multipurpose numerical prediction model designed to simulate atmospheric conditions. In its turn, BRAMS differs from RAMS due to the development of computational modules more suitable to tropical atmospheres.

The primary objective of BRAMS is to provide a single model to Brazilian Regional Weather Centers. However, many regional centers in Brazil execute mesoscale forecasts in their geographical area. Figure 1 shows, as an output example, results of BRAMS execution in the south region of Brazil, these results are related to accumulated precipitation in this region.

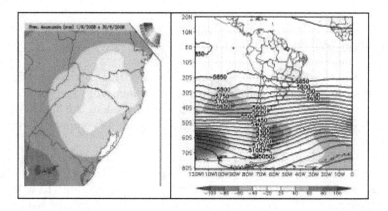

Fig. 1. BRAMS execution results over the south region of Brazil.

On a daily basis, an operational climate forecast with 5 km of spatial resolution is regularly done by the CPTEC/INPE for the entire South American territory using BRAMS in a supercomputer. Outcomes of this forecast are then used as initial and boundary conditions to perform more detailed forecasts, for different regions of Brazil.

4   Porting BRAMS to the Cloud

In this section, we describe the execution model of the application and the requirements to perform its simulations. We also present the architecture developed to run in Azure and the challenges and solutions we provided based on our findings.

One of the objectives of the porting procedures was to automatize the process to create in a reproducible way new cloud versions of BRAMS each time a new version of the source code is released. With the previous requisite in mind, we decided that the best way to achieve this was by performing the minimal amount of modifications to the application. BRAMS is an application coded in Fortran language composed of more than 350000 lines of code and more than 500 source code files. BRAMS uses MPI for the communication between its processes.

4.1 Challenges and Solutions

The source codes provided for HPC applications often lack good documentation, code comments and most of the time has been optimized for a very specific type of machine or architecture. This code requires several modifications to run on commodity machines. These characteristics create a situation in which porting a complete application becomes a lengthy and not so trivial task. The purpose of this work was to port the BRAMS application with minimal modifications to a cloud infrastructure to allow future upgrades based on new versions of the source code released by the CPTEC.

Another challenge to port this kind of application to the cloud is the access to the filesystem compared to a grid environment. In a grid, it is common the usage of a network storage device or a distributed file system. The storage model of Microsoft Azure allows the storage of files in objects called blobs or in tables. The usage of one of the previous models required an intrusive modification of one optimized mechanism of BRAMS. We opted to use a distributed filesystem to store the input data for the simulations and to store all the output files.

In a cloud environment, to reduce the usage cost is necessary to automate most of the task related to the creation of an initial instance ready to begin processing. Due to the way the cloud services are charged, the time and resources spent configuring, compiling and getting the instance up to the point of being saved as base for future instances has to be taken into account. This process must be completely automated to allow a complete pay-as-you-go usage of BRAMS in Azure.

4.2 System Architecture of BRAMS in the Cloud

Figure 2 depicts the architecture of the ported application. An user performs all the required commands in an interactive way directly over a frontend instance. This frontend VM instance manages the operations required to create the number of VM instances required, and that are available for the service. Each one of those instances has a working copy of BRAMS with all the necessary configuration to respond to orders generated by the frontend and with access to the distributed filesystem. The processing instances are created on-demand when a new job is received, after finishing processing, they are deleted. Another approach with the processing instances was to create the instances and leave them stopped while there is nothing else to process, and starting again when a new job arrives, basically an allocation-deallocation process.

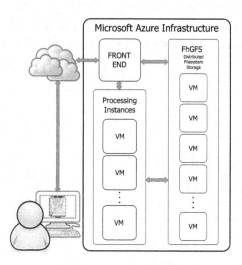

Fig. 2. Overview of BRAMS system architecture in Microsoft Azure.

Data Sources. The execution of BRAMS requires the download of input data to create the initial conditions and satellite data pre-processed by the CPTEC using their global and regional model. The download site is an FTP server with input data of fires, chemistry, soil moisture, sea surface temperature and others. The data is downloaded and processed in the first stage of the application workflow.

This initial step must be taken into account before running any simulation. In a cloud service, the cost of data transfer and data storage is billed in a different way. Microsoft Azure does not charge for input transfer, but charges for the storage. We decided to keep this input data to use it in future experiments preventing unnecessary data transfer. The input data transfer is not charged but requires an instance to perform this procedure in a scheduled way based on the publication of new data. The service VM frontend was assigned to this task because it is an instance running continuously. This instance will be managing the complete workflow of the simulations.

This input data must be converted to the format used by BRAMS. The first step in a simulation is to check that files needed have been downloaded and converted. The frontend also performs the converting step after the download of input data has finished.

Execution Model. In this subsection, the execution model of BRAMS in Azure is described in a timeline fashion. Upon receiving an order to start a new execution of BRAMS, the frontend begins a series of steps as presented on Fig. 3. The first step is to start the resource allocation of the BRAMS processing nodes. This step performs a check on the distributed storage system and in parallel starts or creates the computing intensive instances (based on the type of experiment).

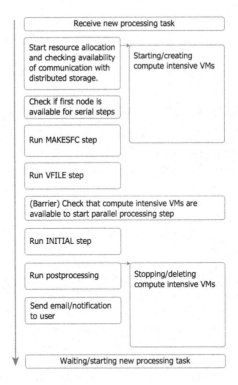

Fig. 3. BRAMS workflow in Microsoft Azure.

One BRAMS execution consists of three main steps to generate forecasts. The first one is called MAKESFC. In this step the global data files of soil type, sea surface temperature and topography are converted to files that cover only the area that is going to be forecasted. This step is sequential, because of this only one process performs this step in the workflow of the application; usually the first compute instance. The second step, MAKEVFILE, generates files with the initial and boundary conditions of each grid in the area to be analyzed for the integration(forecasting) time. This step is also sequential.

At this point, the workflow stops to check if the creation of the compute nodes has been successful and has ended. If the conditions allow it, the workflow continues with the third step that is the actual simulation and forecast. This step is called INITIAL, and it uses the number of processors available based on the number of compute instances. This number of VMs is passed to the MPI call that starts the BRAMS executable.

After the forecasting has finished, a post-processing step should be performed on the output data to visualize the forecasts results. This step is also sequential and is performed by the frontend. In parallel to this step, the frontend sends a stop or delete command (depending on the experiment) to the compute nodes to free resources and stop being billed for their usage.

At the end of the post-processing step, a user notification is sent to their machine if it is still logged on and to an email provided at the beginning of the simulation. Finally, the frontend checks that all the compute VMs are in the expected stopped or delete state and waits for the next forecast execution.

5   Experimental Methodology and Environment

To compare the performance of BRAMS in a cloud environment, we executed a series of experiments in a local cluster and compared it with the version running on the Azure platform. The tests were performed scaling the number of nodes available. The experiment consisted in perform the same simulation five times using 8 more CPU cores at every iteration up to 64 CPU cores. With this test, we intended to compare the performance of the Azure instances versus real hardware in a local cluster. The test allowed to check the scalability of BRAMS in those two environments and help to identify different issues.

HPC applications require low latency values, in the following experiment we collected information on this topic using 8 compute nodes and getting their latencies and the number of hops between them. The experiment consisted of two scenarios with two types of network analysis. The first one created 8 BRAMS instances and analyzed the hops between each node and from the frontend to the 8 instances, in this case, the frontend was a VM already instantiated. After the check, the VMs were deleted and created again. The same process was repeated five times for all the 8 VMs. In the second scenario, the VMs were not deleted but stopped. The Azure VM managing mechanism could reallocate in different physical machines the instances that are stopped when started again. We wanted to analyze the latencies in those cases too.

In a final experiment, we analyzed the time spent in usual deployment operations of a cloud service, namely start, stop, delete and create instances. The time spent in this operations affect the costs of running a cluster service on-demand because the machines are deallocated at the end of each session. We notice that those kind of operations in Azure blocked the subscription from performing another task. It seems like those operations are performed in a serial fashion. The time it takes to perform these operations affect the expected time of the experiments. We wanted to know who much time was spent on each operation.

Table 1. Hardware details of the machine used for the performance experiments.

	Local cluster	Cloud
Machine type	Rack Server	Azure VM Instance Standard A4
Processor	Intel Xeon E5310@1.60 GHZ	Intel Xeon E5-2660@2.20 GHz
Memory	8 GB	14 GB
HDD	250 GB + 250 GB	29 GB + 281 GB
Distributed storage	FhGFS	FhGFS
Networking	Gigabit	Gigabit

5.1 Machines

The environments and characteristics of each machine used in our experiments on the cloud cluster and the local cluster are described in this section.

(1) Microsoft Azure IaaS cloud: Azure offers multiple options regarding IaaS. To minimize communications overhead in the HPC application we use the larger Linux instance sizes, available for our Azure subscription. We use the Extra-large compute instance. This instance (A4)[1] consists of 8 CPU cores running at 2.20 GHz and with 14 GB of memory. The advertised bandwidth available in the network interconnection for this instance size is 800 Mbps. The storage was provided by 8 A3 instances each one with 1TB disk using the Fraunhofer Parallel File System, FhGFS[2].

(2) Real Machines: Each machine consists of two Intel Xeon E5310 Processors, each one with four cores running at 1.60 GHz and 8 GB, Interconnected by a Gigabit switch. The storage was provided by four computer nodes of the same characteristics but not involved in processing. Each one those storage nodes with 500 GB using the Fraunhofer Parallel File System, FhGFS.

A summary of the hardware details of the machines used and characteristics are depicted in Table 1.

6 Evaluation Results

This section presents the results of our experiments. First, we show the and analyze the results of the performance experiments. The experiment consisted of executing BRAMS to perform a forecast of 72 h using a grid resolution of 50 km covering a square perimeter of 6000 km. In the second part, we present our findings regarding the network latencies. Finally we analyze the overhead created by the cloud operations, creating instances, destroying them or starting and stopping their execution.

6.1 Performance

Performance results of BRAMS execution are shown in Fig. 4. The experiment started with one 8 CPU cores.Was progressively growing by adding in each step a VM instance with 8 CPU cores in the case of Azure.Adding one more node at each step in the local cluster, going up to 64 CPU cores. Figure 4 show the average execution time of 5 runs of the INITIAL step in the forecast simulation for each number of nodes and instances.

With 8 processes, it took 6828,54 s for the local cluster and 6553, 84 for the Azure instance to finish the forecast, almost 300 s difference. In the first three tests, the Local cluster took longer to finish the forecast. The Azure instances

---

[1] http://msdn.microsoft.com/en-us/library/azure/dn197896.aspx.
[2] http://fhgfs.com.

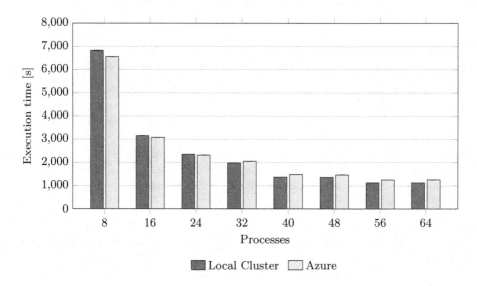

Fig. 4. Performance depicts execution time of a 72 h integration forecast running on the local cluster and on the cloud instances, horizontal axis shows the number of processes.

finished first by a small margin in these three cases, 4 %, 2 %, and 1 % respectively. The frequency difference between the machines is noticeable, being 37, 5 % higher in the advertised value for the A4 Azure instance, but this fact did not reflect any advantage for the Azure instance.

In the following five tests, the Azure cluster was slower by 4 %, 8 %, 8 %, 11 % and 11 %. A trend in performance loss.

It is important to remark that BRAMS is a CPU bound application with a high amount of communication between processes. For this reason, we expected to encounter a performance degradation due to virtualization. We found that, in this case, the amount of degradation was higher than expected.

The variability of this experiments was small, around 2,92 s on average on Azure, a 0,16 percent, and 1,43 s on the local cluster, 0,05 percent. These results and their consistency shows that BRAMS behavior was consistent between experiments and that is possible to scale up to a certain point using the Azure infrastructure even with the penalty imposed by the virtualization overhead.

6.2   Network Latency

Regarding network latencies, we obtain an average of 70 μs with a 24 % standard deviation. The results of this experiment are shown in Fig. 5. Reallocation of nodes generated higher latencies than creating new instances. The latencies between the nodes were in most cases lower than with the frontend. The number of hops between nodes was consistent, four hops in 99 % of the cases.

Contrasting with the network latency obtained in Azure, the local cluster had an average latency of 12 μs. For HPC applications like BRAMS, the latency

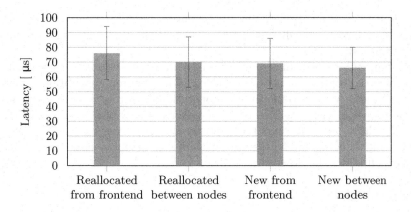

Fig. 5. Network Latency between the nodes and the frontend.

in Azure network impacts the scalability and performance. This latency creates a major issue for the deployment of larger BRAMS simulations in Azure. The latencies in this tightly coupled application limit the possibility of run bigger experiments due to the losses in communications compared with the gains in raw processing power.

6.3 Cloud Operations

The time spent in cloud managing operations is shown on Fig. 6. The time spent in node creation is more than twice the time of the other three operations. This behavior could be due to a situation generated by the command line tools of Azure. In the command line is not possible to instantiate a virtual machine and add it to a running service without assigning an ssh endpoint, even if the instance

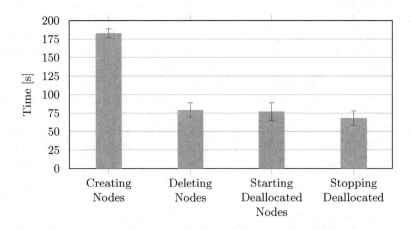

Fig. 6. Time spent on the deployment operations in the cloud service

is not going to use it this endpoint. Regarding security concerns, we proceed to delete the endpoint immediately. This operation halts the creation of new nodes until it finishes.

We found a high variability in the time spent by these operations, up to 16 % in the case of stopping nodes. The fact that the Azure subscription is locked each time the services is performing an operation could prevent the deployment of larger experiments that instantiate a larger amount of machines. The time it would take to start an hypothetic large number of virtual machines versus would be higher compared with executing with less virtual machines, is a possible scenario caused by the described behavior.

7   Conclusions

In this paper we present our findings in running an HPC application in a cloud computing infrastructure using IaaS. We compared the performance between execution in a cluster with real machines versus a cluster in the cloud. Experiments show that it is possible to run HPC applications in Azure reducing most of the configuration work. The performance show that azure offers possibilities to move applications from legacy code and that it is possible to replicate a cluster while reducing the complexity to run HPC applications in Microsoft Azure.

The overhead created by latencies and the time spent in operations not related to actual usage could impose an adoption barrier to further analyze HPC applications in azure. This overhead creates a non processing state in which the VMs already started are waiting to start processing but waiting noticeable amounts of time before perform useful computation. In this waiting state all the idle VMs generate costs that are expected to be reduce by the usage of a cloud infrastructure. Variability between experiments was low in Azure, this characteristic is important for HPC.

The performance gap in the two environments presented, based in the advertised characteristics of the virtual instances should be perceivable. By performing an experiment comparing a 2006 CPU like the one inside the local machines against a 2012 CPU in an Azure instance a remarkable performance gap was expected. Obtaining similar performance between those CPUs shows clearly that there is space to improve the processing performance of the cloud service provided by Microsoft. Even with some of the inconveniences found, cloud computing is a promising alternative getting better as time passes. As long as providers upgrade their hardware driven by the competitive market and keep lowering the prices of their services.

For the future, we intend to perform a full analysis of the cost of running a simulation of BRAMS. We also will capture more metrics to cover all the aspects of the execution and try to improve the performance of this HPC application in a cloud environment.

Acknowledgments. The authors would like to thank the CPTEC by their help. This research has been partially supported by the CNPq, CAPES, Microsoft and the HPC4E project.

References

1. Truong, H.L., Dustdar, S.: Cloud computing for small research groups in computational science and engineering: current status and outlook. Computing **91**(1), 75–91 (2011)
2. Yang, X., Wallom, D., Waddington, S., Wang, J., Shaon, A., Matthews, B., Wilson, M., Guo, Y., Guo, L., Blower, J.D., Vasilakos, A.V., Liu, K., Kershaw, P.: Cloud computing in e-science: research challenges andopportunities. J. Supercomput. **70**(1), 408–464 (2014)
3. Benedict, S.: Performance issues and performance analysis tools for hpc cloud applications: a survey. Computing **95**(2), 89–108 (2013)
4. Roloff, E., Diener, M., Carissimi, A., Navaux, P.: High performance computing in the cloud: deployment, performance and cost efficiency. In: IEEE 4th International Conference on Cloud Computing Technology and Science (CloudCom), pp. 371–378, December 2012
5. Langmead, B., Schatz, M., Lin, J., Pop, M., Salzberg, S.: Searching for SNPs with cloud computing. Genome Biol. **10**(11) (2009)
6. Evangelinos, C., Hill, C.N.: Cloud computing for parallel scientific HPC applications: feasibility of running coupled atmosphere-ocean climate models on Amazon's EC2. In: The 1st Workshop on Cloud Computing and its Applications (CCA) (2008)
7. Johnston, S., Cox, S., Takeda, K.: Scientific computation and data management using microsoft windows azure. In: Fiore, S., Aloisio, G. (eds.) Grid and Cloud Database Management, pp. 169–192. Springer, Heidelberg (2011)
8. Lu, W., Jackson, J., Barga, R.: AzureBlast: a case study of developing science applications on the cloud. In: Proceedings of the 19th ACM International Symposium on High Performance Distributed Computing, HPDC 2010, pp. 413–420. ACM, New York (2010)
9. Simalango, M., Oh, S.: Feasibility study and experience on using cloud infrastructure and platform for scientific computing. In: Furht, B., Escalante, A. (eds.) Handbook of Cloud Computing, pp. 535–551. Springer, New York (2010)
10. CPTEC-INPE: Brazilian Regional Atmospheric Modelling System (BRAMS). http://www.cptec.inpe.br/brams. Accessed 10 August 2014
11. Pielke, R., Cotton, W., Walko, R., Tremback, C., Lyons, W., Grasso, L., Nicholls, M., Moran, M., Wesley, D., Lee, T., Copeland, J.: A comprehensive meteorological modeling system - RAMS. Meteorol. Atmos. Phys. **49**(1–4), 69–91 (1992)

Determining the Real Capacity
of a Desktop Cloud

Carlos E. Gómez[1,2(✉)], César O. Díaz[1], César A. Forero[1],
Eduardo Rosales[1], and Harold Castro[1]

[1] Systems and Computing Engineering Department, School of Engineering,
Universidad de Los Andes, Bogotá, Colombia
{ce.gomez10, co.diaz, ca.forero10,
ee.rosales24, hcastro}@uniandes.edu.co
[2] Universidad del Quindío, Armenia, Colombia

Abstract. Computer laboratories at Universities are underutilized most of the
time [1]. Having an averaged measure of its computing resources usage would
allow researchers to harvest the capacity available by deploying opportunistic
infrastructures, that is, infrastructures mostly supported by idle computing
resources which run in parallel to tasks performed by the resource owner
(end-user). In this paper we measure such usage in terms of CPU and RAM. The
metrics were obtained by using the SIGAR library on 70 desktops belonging to
two independent laboratories during the three busiest weeks in the semester. We
found that the averaged usage of CPU is less than 5 % while RAM is around
25 %. The results show that in terms of the amount of floating point operations
per second (FLOPS) there is a capacity of 24 GFLOPS that can be effectively
harvest by deploying opportunistic infrastructures to support e-Science without
affecting the performance perceived by end-users and avoiding underutilization
and the acquisition of new hardware.

1 Introduction

Computer laboratories at universities usually have a computing capacity superior than
the one demanded by end-users to perform their daily activities then leading to its
underutilization [1]. Such idle capacity in each desktop could be harvest by deploying
opportunistic infrastructures. Those are infrastructures mostly supported by idle computing resources and are based on agents and/or virtual machines that run in parallel to
tasks performed by the end-user. In our university campus we use UnaCloud [2], a
desktop cloud able to opportunistically execute clusters of customized and isolated
virtual machines that harvest idle computing resources to support e-Science projects.
Off-the-shelf, distributed, non-dedicated, and heterogeneous computing resources
available on desktops from computer laboratories mostly support this execution. In
order to determine the real capacity available in such laboratories it is necessary to
measure its usage metrics.

A previous study performed in 2011 [3] had similar objectives. However, such
desktops have been fully replaced and, as expected, the new devices are equipped with
modern technologies. The new features introduced in such recent hardware has

C. Osthoff et al. (Eds.): CARLA 2015, CCIS 565, pp. 62–72, 2015.
DOI: 10.1007/978-3-319-26928-3_5

motivated some concerns, particularly, the ones present in fourth generation processors because they have an impact on the CPU usage [4], along with RAM memory access. New hardware includes processors, main boards, RAM memory, and network interface cards, among others. However, the most of the applications that use UnaCloud are CPU – and/or RAM– intensive and thus it is the sole scope of this research.

The data collected to conduct this research was gathered through and extension of UnaCloud which main function was to periodically monitor usage variables on the physical machines where it executes. However, this monitoring component can be also executed independently in order to measure usage of any desktop or computer laboratory. For this purpose, the SIGAR (System Information Gatherer And Reporter) API [5], a specialized software tool to build monitoring systems was used. We collected information about the usage of two computer laboratories with 70 computers. Data collection was performed during the three busiest weeks in the semester in order to have a representative sample of its utilization by students. The results show that the average utilization of each computer remains in values lower than 5 % in CPU and around 25 % of their RAM when students are performing their daily activities. In the end, we determined the amount of FLOPS could run each computer by LinpackJava [6].

As a result of this research, we can know the actual possibilities of using UnaCloud without affecting the performance perceived by users and the amount of FLOPS as a metric established that specifies the capacity of each computer laboratory to support the implementation of some academic or research project based on desktop cloud.

The remainder of this paper is organized as follows. Section 2 presents a background about the main subject of the paper. Section 3 covers the related work. Section 4 shows the methodology used to conduct this research. Experimental setup and results are addressed in Sects. 5 and 6. The paper finalizes with conclusions future work in Sect. 7. In the end, we determined the amount of FLOPS could run each computer by LinpackJava [6].

2   Background

In this section, relevant concepts are introduced to contextualize this research work, namely desktop grid/cloud, UnaCloud, performance, cloud monitoring, metrics, the SIGAR API and the modern processors technologies.

2.1   Desktop Grid/Cloud

Desktop grids are a well-known strategy to provide large-scale computing infrastructures by taking advantage of idle computing resources mainly available on desktops. There are two recognized approaches to build desktop grids. First, the approach based on stand-alone agents directly installed as applications on top of the operating system. Second, the approach based on virtualization technologies. In the first approach, the agents identify idle computing resources in order to harvest them by executing jobs. BOINC [7], SETI@home [8], SZTAKI [9] and OurGrid [10], among others are examples of such agent-based desktop grids. In the second approach, through type II hypervisors it is used virtualization to deploy on-demand instances of virtual machines on off-the-shelf desktops. That is, hypervisors are able to provide virtualization features on the top of a host operating system. Some virtualization-based desktop grids are LHC@Home [11], CernVM [12], GBAC [13], and UnaCloud [2]. However, UnaCloud is conceptually a desktop cloud. That is, a Cloud Computing Infrastructure as a Service (IaaS) implementation, which provides basic computing resources (processing, storage, and networking) to run arbitrary software, including operating systems and applications. Such implementation provides customized features that meet complex computing requirements similarly to a Cloud IaaS supported by dedicated and robust infrastructures. Nevertheless, UnaCloud is mostly supported by off-the-shelf, distributed, non-dedicated, and heterogeneous computing resources (such as desktops) available in computer laboratories that are part of different administrative domains in a University Campus.

2.2   UnaCloud

UnaCloud is an opportunistic model aimed to provide computing resources taking advantage of idle computing resources available in a university campus [2]. UnaCloud is formed by two components: the server and the agent. The server is a Web application, which receives cloud-users requests. Consequently, the UnaCloud server provides services such as virtual machine image management, provision, configuration, and the deployment of virtual machine clusters, monitoring and general physical infrastructure management according to cloud-users profiles. UnaCloud agent is a lightweight, highly portable and easy to install program that is executed on each desktop to use idle computing resources in a non-intrusive manner. The agent responsibilities include initiating, restarting, cloning and stopping virtual machines.

2.3   Performance

The definition of performance depends on the metric used to measure it. For example, response time (the time required to complete a task), and throughput (the number of tasks finished per unit of time) are two common performance metrics [14].

On the other hand, it is called FLOPS (FLoating-point Operation per Second) a sequence of mathematical operations that involves the use of floating point numbers achieved by cores within processors in a second. A core can perform a certain number of FLOPS per clock cycle, which is measured in hertz (Hz). A processor can do 4 FLOPS per Hz. Given that the internal clock speed of the cores and its amount are features of the processor, it is possible to calculate a theoretical performance of a processor [15]. For example, suppose that a 3.4-GHz processor has 8 cores. Then, it can achieve $4 \times 3.4 \times 10^9$ FLOPS equals to 13.6 GFLOPS per core. To exemplify the computing power of a desktop grid, SETI@home published in [16], has an average 682.820 TeraFLOPS.

2.4   Cloud Monitoring

Cloud monitoring is an essential function of the cloud management system. Providers need to keep everything related with IT infrastructure under control in order to make decisions about the cloud services. This includes datacenter and performance management, troubleshooting, billing, and security, etc. [17]. According to [18], there are two abstraction levels related with cloud monitoring: high-level and low-level. High-level monitoring refers to the virtual platform status. Information about high-level is gathered by the provider, consumer or external applications. This monitoring information is more relevant for consumers than for providers. Low-level monitoring refers to physical platform status, that is datacenter, hardware, operating system, network and security information. Given that this information is about the provider facilities, it is not disclosed to the general public. Cloud monitoring allows the cloud management department to measure the infrastructure and applications behavior in terms of several metrics, which depend of the abstraction level, and each provider. As a result, other aspects can be managed, such as Service Level Agreements. On the other hand, customers also need information about their applications.

2.5   Metrics

A metric is the fundamental concept in any monitoring system. In the cloud computing context for example, a metric is specific information that the cloud manager requires to collect in order to obtain statistics about the general or particular behavior of a cloud service. Most metrics are measured in function of time and are collected at regular intervals. The most common metrics are CPU usage, RAM usage, the information sent and received and latency. CPU and RAM usage are used in this study and are defined as follows.

CPU Used. It is the percentage of time spent processing the instructions needed to complete a task. This metric is a very common method to evaluate the performance of a physical machine [19]. *100 % − CPU Usage* is the CPU Idle, in other words, the percentage of time the processor is not used.

RAM Used. It is the percentage of RAM associated with a running process.

2.6   SIGAR API

There are several monitoring platforms and tools, commercial and open source [17]. Some examples of commercial platforms or tools are CloudWatch, AzureWatch, CloudStatus, and NewRelic. Some examples of open source platforms are Nagios, CloudHarmony, and SIGAR, the API used to support this study.

SIGAR (System Information Gatherer And Reporter) provides an interface for gathering system information such as memory (system-wide and per-process), file system and network. It also provides an API to obtain a lot of metrics. It can be used in several operating systems and several programming languages although it is implemented in C. SIGAR is a free software project licensed under the Apache License, Version 2.0 [5].

2.7   Modern Processor Technologies

Fourth generation processors technologies include Turbo Boost, Hyper-Threading, and SpeedStep. Turbo Boost allows the processor to increase the base operating frequency at runtime reaching higher performance dynamically based on parameters such as the core temperature, the type of workload, and the number of active cores [20]. With Hyper-Threading, processors can run more than one thread in parallel. As a result, it is more efficient to run multithread applications by activating this feature [21]. The SpeedStep technology enables the processor to reach greater performance metrics increasing its clock speed. Thus, the average temperature and the average energy consumption are reduced [22].

3   Related Work

Several studies have been conducted in order to analyze the availability of one or more computers to determine whether it is possible to use their idle resources to execute a desktop grid/cloud on them.

Kondo et al. [23] presented a paper about the usage of application-level traces of four real desktop grids for simulation and modeling. Moreover, authors describe statistics that reflect the heterogeneity and volatility of desktop grid resources. Finally, they use a metric to quantify the utility of the desktop grid for task-parallel applications.

Mutka [24] in 1992, Yaik et al. [25] in 2006, and Shafazand et al. [26] and Gan Chee [27] in 2014 predicted the opportunity to take advantage of idleness in computational resources using different techniques. In [24], the paper highlights workstation usage patterns in cluster management and analyzes them in order to identify opportunities for exploiting idle capacity. The study is based on end-user activity traces in a university environment with the aim of making good predictions in order to schedule time-limited jobs. Meanwhile, the authors of [25] try to determine opportunities to harness the idle resources of a computer using a suffix tree to find out patterns in the CPU usage. On the other hand [26] proposes a recommendation model used by the allocation scheduler to forecast the availability of a computer in a desktop grid. Finally, in [27] authors devise a framework to predict which workstations can be used as part of an ad hoc computer cluster and when this can be done. The authors say that the success of an ad hoc computer cluster depends on the usage characteristics of the computers because of the variable workstations turn-on duration.

Dominguez et al. in 2005 [1] quantified the usage of main resources (CPU, main memory, disk space, and network bandwidth) on machines from classroom laboratories running Windows 2000. These authors measured several indicators about main resources and usage habits, especially for interactive user sessions at the computer causing high rates of idleness in computational resources. In the end, the results obtained suggest that desktop grids can be executed on those infrastructures.

Oviedo in 2011 [2] presented a Master thesis about bioinformatics in which UnaCloud is used as High Performance Computing infrastructure. In this work, the author includes a first study to determine the average behavior of physical machines when UnaCloud was executed and to identify the physical machine with the greatest chance of being restarted. The study included a metric of free CPU percentage and the unavailability times caused by restarting and shutting down the computers.

Regarding to the Oviedo's work, we include RAM as an additional measure, and we also applied the Linpack benchmark for getting the total capacity of the laboratories. We also developed a monitoring system that not only helped us to obtain the information that was used in this study, but also it can be used to monitor the execution of UnaCloud permanently. Thus, we will obtain permanent statistics that can be used to make decisions about UnaCloud use.

4 Methodology

The main goal of this research is to obtain updated and accurate information about the regular activities of students in the computer laboratories where UnaCloud is executed. This will allow us to determine metrics about the underutilized resources of computers in terms of CPU and RAM. In particular, we are interested in determining not only the idle computational power that can be harvested without disturbing the end-user of a physical machine, but also the aggregate capacity, measured in FLOPS, of a campus based on computer laboratories to support projects of the academic and scientific community.

4.1 Monitoring Component Developed

To collect the data concerning the aforementioned variables, we implemented a monitoring component that is part of the UnaCloud Agent. This component is running constantly and is responsible for collecting data at a frequency that can be specified. Although this module is part of UnaCloud, it can be run independently.

The monitoring component was developed using Java 7 and includes the services provided by SIGAR API version 1.6.4 [5]. This component gains access to the main operating system variables and stores them in a text file on each computer. The agent periodically sends the records to a database. Given the volume of monitoring data that is generated and the lack of relationship among them, a non-relational database was selected.

The monitoring tool includes a mechanism for data recovery in case of failure, which identifies whether a problem with sending the last data file has occurred. There is also a strategy based on random times to avoid concurrent access by the agents to the database, which might lead to bottlenecks.

This monitoring system can be managed from the UnaCloud management console. This console enables or disables the monitoring for a particular machine or a complete laboratory. In addition, it is possible to configure a report generator indicating which machines or laboratories and the desired time range to be included in the report. The system currently generates reports in comma separated values (CSV) format. Data is then imported into Microsoft Excel for graphical statistics analysis.

4.2   Hardware Testbed

The two monitored computer laboratories for this study (Waira 1 and Waira 2) are used by the Systems and Computing Engineering Department at Universidad de Los Andes to support courses of different subjects in undergraduate and postgraduate levels. Besides, these computers are also used by students to develop their academic activities when no classes are scheduled. The laboratories are configured with Windows 7 Enterprise 64-bits (Service Pack 1) as unique host operating system. Each laboratory has 35 computers with Intel Core(TM) i7-4770 CPU @ 3.40 GHz x8 processor, 16 GB of RAM, and 500 GB hard disk. A Gigabit Ethernet LAN interconnects all computers.

4.3   Data Gathered

Similar to what Domingues [1] presented, we obtained both static and dynamic information. Static information includes processor specifications (name, type, and frequency), RAM and hard disk size and operating system (name and version), among others. Dynamic information is related with the computer usage during the day. We obtained information on CPU and RAM usage.

4.4   Data Analysis

From the information gathered by the monitoring component developed, the daily average CPU utilization and the average daily use of RAM were calculated. In addition, we used LinpackJava [25], a well-known benchmark, to determine the amount of FLOPS could run each computer. From this indicator, the total capacity of an entire laboratory is estimated. Furthermore, the rates of utilization of CPU and RAM were analyzed to identify changes in end-user behavior at different times of the day.

4.5   Limitations

One difficulty we experienced was the loss of monitoring information because carrying out administrative tasks such as installing software or updating the operating system by authorized personnel. Students can restart the computers as well causing the same effect. Moreover, although sporadic, it may occur that an end-user leaves the session open, meaning that the monitoring information indicates that the end-user is utilizing the machine but with an occupancy level of minimum resources, which affect the results.

5   Experimental Setup

Based on the study conducted in 2011 [3], it can be assumed that the computer laboratories under study are underutilized most of the time. However, it is needed to have updated and reliable metrics to determine the real capacity for the execution of the current desktop cloud. To reach that, it is essential to identify the amount of underutilized resources of computers in terms of CPU and RAM. Furthermore, it is needed to determine the aggregate capacity in FLOPS. Therefore, we pose two scenarios, described in Fig. 1, for the collection of data from 7:00 am to 10:00 pm, time in which the laboratories serve students.

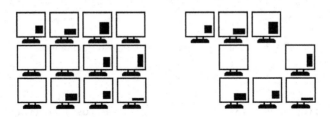

Fig. 1. Test scenarios.

Figure 1(A) represents the scenario #1. In this case, we took we took into account 70 computers in order to measure the average laboratory usage. This is the reference point for calculating the total capacity of the laboratory measured in FLOPS. For scenario #2, we only considered the computers where a student was seated in front of them, as represents it the Fig. 1(B). This scenario allows us to determine what users consume taking into account the two metrics analyzed in this study.

6 Experimental Results

Statistical charts show graphical results of an average day obtained from experiments because the results are very similar. In the end, we present the capacity of each laboratory measured in FLOPS. A point on a graph represents the average of all measurements taken every minute from 7:00 am until 10:00 pm.

The figures presented in this section summarize the results for the aforementioned tests scenarios. All figures use the CPU or RAM percentage in the Y-axis, and the time (hours of the day) in the X-axis. Figure 2 shows the CPU consumption, while Fig. 3 shows RAM consumption on Waira Lab.

As shown in Fig. 2(A), most values in scenario 1 are less than 3 %. This indicates that the lab has low CPU utilization level. Figure 2(B) shows the scenario #2 behavior where the usage is not significant. In this scenario, gaps occurred when there is no user. Gathered data indicate that the use of laboratories is not significant, leading to a great opportunity for implementing a desktop cloud without disturbing the activities of students.

Figure 3(A and B) has similar behavior in the four scenarios of our tests. Waira Labs has RAM consumption between 19 % and 31 %, which corresponds to availability between 69 % and 81 %. These data indicate that the lab has a low level of use in RAM.

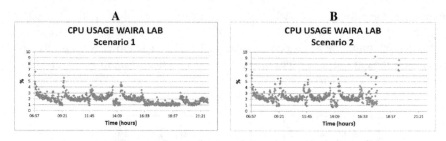

Fig. 2. Scenario #1. Waira Lab CPU Consumption.

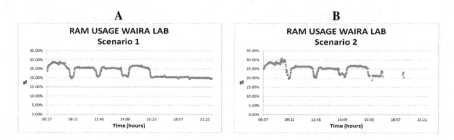

Fig. 3. Waira Lab RAM Consumption.

On the other hand, after applying the LinpackJava benchmark [6]. We run the benchmarking on 70 computers of Waira Labs. The result was 343,3 MFLOPS each one. Therefore, the total capacity is the product of multiplying 343,3 MFLOPS by 70 resulting 24 GFLOPS. This is the aggregate capacity labs.

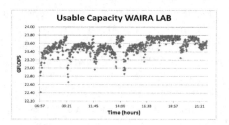

Fig. 4. Total capacity of Waira Lab.

As expected, the total available capacity of the laboratory is a measure that changes during the day. This measure is calculated based on the CPU usage of the Waira laboratories. The results shown in Fig. 4 indicate that most of the values are between 23 and 24 GLOFPS.

7 Conclusion and Future Work

Although it is known that the computer laboratories at universities are underutilized most of the time, we wanted to have a current measure of that utilization level. UnaCloud, our desktop cloud was developed to take advantage of idle computing power of these kinds of labs. However, the lack of an updated report on the amount of the available resources in labs prevents to improve indicators of use of UnaCloud. Therefore, we measured the CPU and RAM usage of the Systems and Computer Engineering and Department at Universidad de Los Andes. The tests were performed on 70 desktops belonging to two independent laboratories during the three busiest weeks in the semester. Four scenarios were considered, and the results show that the CPU usage is lower than 3 % most of the time. The RAM usage presented similar results in all scenarios. The average RAM usage is between 19 and 31 %. UnaCloud has exploited the idle capacity of computing resources. However, the results of the tests indicate that there is still an important capacity to grow for the benefit of users UnaCloud, without affecting the performance of the computers used by users to perform their routine activities at the university. On the other hand, the total capacity of the Waira computer labs at our university is significant. Therefore, having a concrete metric in FLOPS allows us to identify the dimensions of the research projects that we can support taking into account our facilities. This situation encourages us to do new tests in order to obtain more conclusive results.

New opportunities have for the future with this investigation. The monitoring component developed can be improved; both in the amount of information obtained from the machines, and automated reporting. It is also necessary to develop a system to measure the impact that UnaCloud has on the user. This would find a way to better use the idle resources in laboratories where UnaCloud running so that it does not interfere with the activities of the students, the main users of the laboratories.

References

1. Domingues, P., Marques, P., Silva, L.: Resource usage of Windows computer laboratories. In: International Conference Workshops on Parallel Processing, ICPP 2005 Workshops, pp. 469–476 (2005)
2. Rosales, E., Castro, H., Villamizar, M.: UnaCloud: opportunistic cloud computing infrastructure as a service. In: CLOUD COMPUTING 2011: the Second International Conference on Cloud Computing, GRIDs, and Virtualization, Rome, Italy (2011)
3. Oviedo, A.: UnaCloud MSA: Plataforma basada en UnaCloud para la generación y análisis de alineamientos múltiples de secuencias. Magister en Ingeneiría, Systems and Computing Engineering, Universidad de Los Andes (2011)
4. Sotelo, G., Rosales, E., Castro, H.: Implications of CPU dynamic performance and energy-efficient technologies on the intrusiveness generated by desktop grids based on virtualization. In: Hernández, G., Barrios Hernández, C.J., Díaz, G., García Garino, C., Nesmachnow, S., Pérez-Acle, T., Storti, M., Vázquez, M. (eds.) CARLA 2014. CCIS, vol. 485, pp. 98–112. Springer, Heidelberg (2014)

5. Morgan, R.: SIGAR -System Information Gatherer And Reporter (2010). https://support. hyperic.com/display/SIGAR/Home
6. Jack, D., Reed, W., Paul, M.: Linpack Benchmark – Java Version (2015). http://www.netlib. org/benchmark/linpackjava/
7. Anderson, D.P.: BOINC: a system for public-resource computing and storage. In: Fifth IEEE/ACM International Workshop on Grid Computing, Proceedings, pp. 4–10 (2004)
8. U. o. California. SETI@home (2015). http://setiathome.ssl.berkeley.edu/
9. SZTAKI (2015). http://szdg.lpds.sztaki.hu/szdg/
10. OurGrid (2013). http://www.ourgrid.org/
11. LHC@home (2014). http://lhcathome.web.cern.ch
12. CernVM Project (2015). http://cernvm.cern.ch/
13. Marosi, A., Kovács, J., Kacsuk, P.: Towards a volunteer cloud system. Future Gener. Comput. Syst. **29**, 1442–1451 (2013)
14. Patterson, D.A., Hennessy, J.L.: Computer Organization and Design: The Hardware/Software Interface, 5th edn. Morgan and Kaufmann, Burlington (2014)
15. Fernandez, M.: Nodes, Sockets, Cores and FLOPS, Oh, My. http://en.community.dell.com/ techcenter/high-performance-computing/w/wiki/2329
16. BOINC. Detailed stats SETI@Home (2015). http://boincstats.com/en/stats/0/project/detail
17. Aceto, G., Botta, A., de Donato, W., Pescapè, A.: Cloud monitoring: a survey. Comput. Netw. **57**, 2093–2115 (2013)
18. Aceto, G., Botta, A., de Donato, W., Pescape, A.: Cloud monitoring: definitions, issues and future directions. In: 2012 IEEE 1st International Conference on Cloud Networking (CLOUDNET), pp. 63–67 (2012)
19. Ahmadi, M.R., Maleki, D.: Performance evaluation of server virtualization in data center applications. In: 2010 5th International Symposium on Telecommunications (IST), pp. 638–644 (2010)
20. Intel Corporation: First the tick, now the tock: Next generation Intel microarchitecture (Nehalem) (2009)
21. Intel Corporation: Intel Turbo Boost Technology in Intel Core Microarchitecture (Nehalem) Based Processors
22. Intel Corporation: Enhanced Intel SpeedStep® Technology - How To Document, 10 April 2015
23. Kondo, D., Fedak, G., Cappello, F., Chien, A.A., Casanova, H.: Characterizing resource availability in enterprise desktop grids. Future Gener. Comput. Syst. **23**, 888–903 (2007)
24. Mutka, M.W.: An examination of strategies for estimating capacity to share among private workstations. In: Presented at the Proceedings of the 1991 ACM SIGSMALL/PC Symposium on Small Systems, Toronto, Ontario, Canada (1991)
25. Yaik, O.B., Chan Huah, Y., Haron, F.: CPU usage pattern discovery using suffix tree. In: The 2nd International Conference on Distributed Frameworks for Multimedia Applications, pp. 1–8 (2006)
26. Shafazand, M., Latip, R., Abdullah, A., Hussin, M.: A model for client recommendation to a desktop grid server. In: Herawan, T., Deris, M.M., Abawajy, J. (eds.) Proceedings of the First International Conference on Advanced Data and Information Engineering (DaEng-2013), vol. 285, pp. 491–498. Springer, Singapore (2014)
27. Gan Chee, T., Ooi Boon, Y., Liew Soung, Y.: Workstations uptime analysis framework to identify opportunity for forming ad-hoc computer clusters. In: 2014 International Conference on Computer, Communications, and Control Technology (I4CT), pp. 234–238 (2014)

Improvements to Super-Peer Policy Communication Mechanisms

Paula Verghelet[1] and Esteban Mocskos[1,2(✉)]

[1] Laboratorio de Sistemas Complejos, Departamento de Computación,
Facultad de Ciencias Exactas y Naturales, Universidad de Buenos Aires,
C1428EGA Buenos Aires, Argentina
{pverghelet,emocskos}@dc.uba.ar
[2] Centro de Simulación Computacional p/Aplic.
Tecnológicas/CSC-CONICET, Godoy Cruz 2390,
C1425FQD Buenos Aires, Argentina

Abstract. The use of large distributed computing infrastructures has become a fundamental component in most of scientific and technological projects. Due to its highly distributed nature, one of the key topics to be addressed in large distributed systems (like Grids and Federation of Clouds) is the determination of the availability and state of resources. Having up-to-date information about resources in the system is extremely important as this is consumed by the scheduler for selecting the appropriate target in each job to be served.

The way in which this information is obtained and distributed is what is known as *Resource Information Distribution Policy*. A centralized organization presents several drawbacks, for example, a single point of failure. Notwithstanding, the static hierarchy has become the defacto implementation of grid information systems.

There is a growing interest in the interaction with the Peer to Peer (P2P) paradigm, pushing towards scalable solutions. Super Peer Policy (SP) is a decentralized policy which presents a notable improvement in terms of response time and expected number of results compared with decentralization one. While Hierarchical policy is valuable for small and medium-sized Grids, SP is more effective in very large systems and therefore is more scalable.

In this work, we analyze SP focusing on the communication between super-peers. An improvement to the standard protocol is proposed which leads to two new SP policies outperforming the standard implementation: N-SP and A2A-SP. These policies are analyzed in terms of obtained performance in Exponential and Barabási network topologies, network consumption and scalability.

1 Introduction

The use of large distributed computing infrastructures has become a fundamental component in most of scientific and technological projects. Just to show some examples, we can mention climate simulation [28], analysis of data generated in

C. Osthoff et al. (Eds.): CARLA 2015, CCIS 565, pp. 73–86, 2015.
DOI: 10.1007/978-3-319-26928-3_6

the experiments of Large Hadron Collider (LHC) [26] and some of the initiatives included in the work of Mattmann et al. [18], like NASA's Planetary Data System, NCI's Early Detection Research Network (NCI-EDRN) and Orbiting Carbon Observatory (OCO), or others Big Data analytics projects mentioned in the work of Assunção et al. [2].

Due to its highly distributed nature, one of the key topics to be addressed in large distributed systems (like Grids and Federation of Clouds) is the determination of the availability and state of resources [6, 7, 24]. Having up-to-date information about resources in the system is extremely important as it is used by the scheduler to select the appropriate target for each job to be served [11, 20].

The way in which this information is obtained and distributed is what is known as *Resource Information Distribution Policy*. In the Grid architecture described by Foster et al. [9], the discovery mechanisms are included in the *Resource Layer*. In the revision of this architecture by Mattmann et al. [18], the information about the state of distributed resources is managed by the *Collective Subsystem*.

The resources that have to be managed by this kind of systems can be characterized in two main classes [23]:

(i) *Static attributes:* the type of attributes which show a very slow rate of change. For example operating system, processor clock frequency, total storage capacity or network bandwidth.

(ii) *Dynamic attributes:* in this class, we can find the attributes related with the use of the system which change as the usage evolves, for example free memory, processor usage, available storage or network usage.

Usually, scheduling a job in a large distributed system involves the coordination of different type of resources and having up-to-date information to guide the selection.

A centralized organization approach presents several drawbacks [23], for example, a single point of failure. The static hierarchy has become the defacto implementation of grid information systems [8]. However, in medium-to-large scale environments, the dynamics of the resource information cannot be captured using a static hierarchy [18, 27]. This approach has similar drawbacks to the centralized one, such as the point of failure and poor scaling for large number of users/providers [21, 22]. Therefore, it results necessary to design new policies for discovery and propagation of resource information.

There is a growing interest in the interaction with the Peer to Peer (P2P) paradigm, pushing towards scalable solutions [16, 27]. These initiatives are base on two common facts: (i) very dynamic and heterogeneous environment and (ii) creation of a virtual working environment by collecting the resources available from a series of distributed, individual entities [22].

Another scenarios in which the resource information is central to an efficient system performance are Volunteer and Mobile Cloud Computing. For example, Ghafarian et al. [10] presents a protocol for resource discovery with QoS restrictions in P2P based volunteer computing systems. While Liu et al. [14] introduces an energy-efficient method of adaptive resource discovery to solve the problem of find how available resources in nearby devices are discovered, it transforms between centralized and flooding modes to save energy.

Iamnitchi et al. [11,12] proposed a P2P approach for organizing the information components in a flat dynamic P2P network. This decentralized approach envisages that every administrative domain maintains its information services and makes it available as part of the P2P network. Schedulers may initiate look-up queries that are forwarded in the P2P network using flooding (a similar approach to the unstructured P2P network Gnutella [25]).

The most common resource information distribution policies are:

- **Random:** Every node chooses randomly another node to query information from. There is no structure at all. Usually this policy is used as baseline behavior to be compare with.
- **Hierarchical:** In this kind of policy, a hierarchy is established beforehand and the resource information is sent using this fixed structure. In this way, the nodes at the top of the hierarchy exchange information with the ones below them. This is the standard actually used by Grids.
- **Super Peer:** Some nodes are defined as *super-peers* working like servers for a subset of nodes and as peers in the network of super-peers. In this way, a two level structure is defined in which the *normal* nodes are only allowed to communicate with a single super-peer and the cluster defined by it. Usually, Random policy is used as the communication policy between the super-peers [11]. When a super-peer receives a query, it first checks the information it has about the nodes that are directly connected to it, if the query can not be solve using this information, the super-peer contacts the others to obtain a response.
- **Best-Neighbor:** Some information about each answer is stored and the next neighbor to query is selected using the quality of the previous answers. At the beginning, the node has no information about its neighbors, thus it chooses randomly. As information is collected, the probability of choosing a neighbor randomly is inversely proportional to the amount of information stored.

Mastroianni et al. [17] evaluated the performance of these policies and analyzed the pros and cons of each solution. In theirs conclusions, the Super Peer Policy (SP) presents a notable improvement in terms of response time and expected number of results, compared with decentralization one, while Hierarchical policy is valuable for small and medium-sized systems, SP is more effective in very large infrastructures therefore is more scalable.

Recently, Cesario et al. [5] studies the performance of a framework oriented to execute applications for distributed data mining combining volunteer computing and P2P architecture. SP policy is used to discover the available resources obtaining an important performance gain compared with standard policy.

In this work, we analyze SP focusing on the communication layer between super-peers. An improvement to the standard communication methodology is proposed which leads to a new SP outperforming the standard implementation.

2   Materials and Methods

To evaluate the different scenarios and policies, we used GridMatrix, an open source tool focused on the analysis of discovery and monitoring information policies, based on SimGrid2 [4].

In despite of the majority of the evaluated aspects of this kind of systems strongly depend on time, it is usually discarded and, as a consequence, limits the analysis of the dynamical nature of the systems. In Mocskos et al. [19] the authors introduced a new set of metrics (Local Information Rate (LIR) and Global Information Rate (GIR)) that incorporate the notion of time decay of information in the evaluation of the system performance:

– **LIR:** captures the amount of information that a particular host has from all the entire system in a single moment. For the host k, LIR_k is:

$$LIR_k = \frac{\sum_{h=1}^{N} f(age_h, expiration_h) \cdot resourceCount_h}{totalResourceCount} \tag{1}$$

  where N is number of hosts in the system, $expiration_h$ is the expiration time of the resources of host h in host k, age_h is the time passed since the information was obtained from that host, $resourceCount_h$ is the amount of resources in host h and $totalResourceCount$ is the total amount of resources in the whole system.
– **GIR:** captures the amount of information that the whole grid knows of itself, calculated as the mean value of every node's LIR.

Two network topologies were analyzed: Exponential and Barabási. Both distribution models are used for connections, where the amount of connections of each node follows an exponential distribution law and power law, commonly seen in the Internet or collaborative networks [1,3].

To setup the scenario for SP policy, GridMatrix partitions the network using `metis` [13]. In each partition, the super-peer is selected minimizing the total distance to the rest of nodes in the partition.

The messages interchanged to inform the state and availability of resources is shown in the Fig. 1. Two types of messages are used: `push` and `poll`. In the stage A of the Fig. 1, the node starts having information about three resources. When this node sends a `push` message to other node (stage B in the same figure), all the information about the resources it knows is communicated to the other node, including the resources belonging to other nodes in the system. All the information has a time-to-live tag that is used to discard it when it gets old. The other type of message is exemplified in stage C and D: a node contacts another one to get information using a `poll` message. After receiving the request (stage C), the node answers the query with a message containing all the information it knows about resources in the system.

In the base implementation of SP, each peer node sends `poll` and `push` messages to a single super-peer. This information is then distributed among the rest of super-peers in the system selecting one each time randomly.

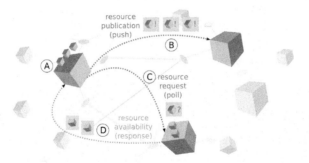

Fig. 1. Messages used to send and receive resource information: `push` (publication of available resources) and `poll` (request of information). A: the host has information about three available resources. B: the node publishes the information about these resources sending a *push* to other node. C: the node request information about resources and sends a *poll* to other node using this message to communicate its own resources. D: the node answers sending the requested information.

As was mentioned before, the Hierarchical policy usually shows the best results [15, 19]. For this reason is used as comparison for the new developed policies in this work.

3 Results

As was previously mentioned, SP generates a two layer hierarchy, the lower layers contains all the nodes which can only communicate with their corresponding super-peer. While in the top layer, we can find all the super-peer which can communicate with the nodes in their assigned partition and with the rest of super-peers.

The standard methodology to communicate among super-peers is using Random Policy. Every period of time (this is one of the configuration parameters of the policy) a `poll` message is sent to a randomly selected super-peer.

Figure 2 presents the behavior of Random Policy variations in exponential topology using 240s as information expiration time. N-Random Policy is similar to standard Random Policy but N messages are sent each time. For example, N-Random N2 sends two messages every time, but to maintain constant the total amount of control messages in the system, the period is also duplicated. Figure 2(a) shows the impact of variation of the time between messages (Refresh time) for N-Random Policy (with $N = 1, 2, 4, 6, 8$) on a 100-node system. As is expected, more messages improves the mean GIR, but it is worth noting that N-Random Policies respond different. In despite of the variation that can be seen in the obtained results, sending more messages could improve the performance of the system.

On the other hand, Fig. 2(b) presents the behavior of N-Random Policy with $N = 8$ compared with standard Random Policy ($N = 1$) and SP using 5 %

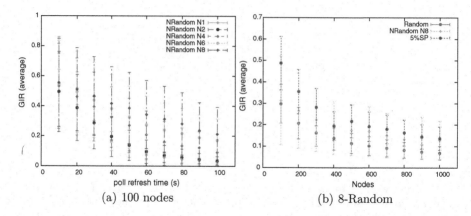

(a) 100 nodes   (b) 8-Random

Fig. 2. Variations of Random Policy in exponential topology. In N-Random Policy more messages are sent each time, but the period is scaled to maintain constant the total amount of interchanged messages at same expiration time. (a) presents mean GIR for $N = 1, 2, 4, 6, 8$ changing the refresh time between `polls`. In (b) the behavior of N-Random Policy (with $N = 8$) is compared against standard Random and Super-Peer using 5 % of super-peers as the size of the system is increased with fixed refresh time.

of super-peers. As expected, SP shows a better mean GIR and slower decrease in the performance as the size of the system increases. The standard Random Policy behaves as expected showing a strong fall in performance with the system size. The N-Random Policy ($N = 8$) or simply N8 shows a better performance in terms of mean GIR, but can not overpass SP.

The observed behavior of N-Random Policy leads to its use as intercommunication protocol between super-peers. The objective for the rest of this work is improving the performance of SP without sacrificing its lack of structure and maintaining its distributed nature by using N-Random Policy.

3.1   N-SP: N-Random Super Peer

N-SP Policy is obtained replacing Random Policy by N-Random as the communication protocol between super-peers. Figure 3 shows the mean GIR for a 200-nodes system with exponential topology and 240 s information expiration time. Three N-SP variations are analyzed with $N = 1, 4, 6$ and different amount of super-peers (i.e. network partitions) 2 %, 5 % and 10 %. In this figure, Hierarchical Policy is included as a reference as this policy usually obtains the best results.

In all the observed cases, standard SP is outperformed by N4-SP and N6-SP. In Fig. 3(a), 2 %SP (standard Super-Peer Policy), N4-SP and N6-SP show almost constant mean GIR as the refresh time of the messages is increased. In Fig. 3(b) and (c), the increment in the refresh time produces a decrease in the mean GIR for all the policies but the impact on standard SP is notoriously stronger than N4-SP and N6-SP. In the three scenarios, N4-SP and N6-SP reach the performance obtained by Hierarchical Policy for refresh times lower than 140 s. In the Fig. 3(c),

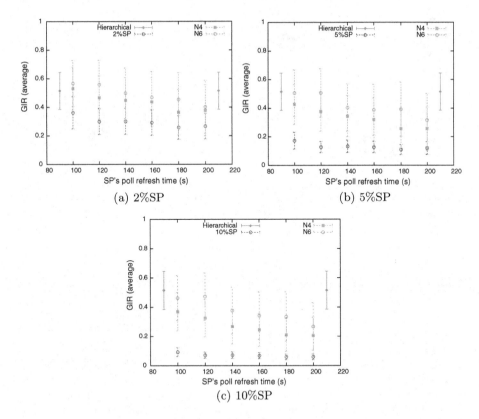

Fig. 3. Super-Peer Policy using N-Random Policy with $N = 1, 4, 6$ for communications between super-peers. Mean GIR obtained while modifying the refresh time in a system with 200 nodes with Exponential topology and different amount of super-peers: (a) 2 %SP, (b) 5 %SP and (c) 10 %SP. Hierarchical Policy is included as a reference.

the system is further partitioned, which means more super-peers. In this case, N6-SP still outperforms N4-SP policy for all the considered refresh times.

To evaluate the behavior of the new policies in terms of bandwidth consumption, the amount of sent messages is analyzed for each one in different scenarios. Figure 4 shows the control messages sent in a fixed period of time (14 h) for two systems of 200 and 500 nodes. These two systems are configured using 5 % (Fig. 4(a) and (c)), and 10 % (Fig. 4(b) and (d)) of super-peers relative to the total present nodes. This figure is obtained using 60 s as the refresh time between peers and in each level of the hierarchy for Hierarchical Policy. The refresh time between super-peers is varied from 100 to 200 s.

As is expected, the total amount of messages increase with the system size for all the studied policies. The variation of the refresh time between super-peers produces almost no change in the case of 200 nodes. When the system size is increased to 500 nodes, N6-SP starts to show strong bandwidth consumption, but N4-SP presents only a slightly increase compared to Hierarchical Policy.

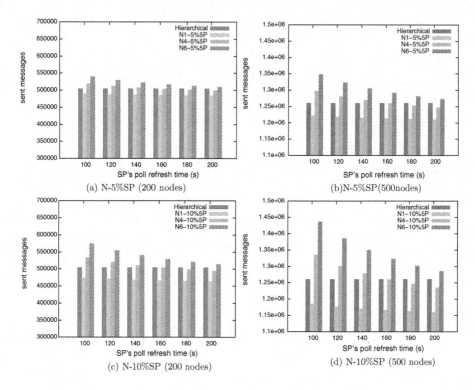

Fig. 4. Control messages sent during 14 h using Hierarchical, N1-SP, N4-SP and N6-SP policies. In (a) and (b) 5 %SP is used, while in (c) and (d) 10 %SP. Two system sizes are considered: 200 nodes in (a) and (c), and 500 nodes in (b) and (d).

To select a variation to be used as the new communication mechanism between super-peers, both aspects should be considered. On one side, the performance obtained as is shown in Fig. 3, which shows N6-SP as the best selection. On the other side, the network usage turns to be the price to be paid to obtain a better performance, as is shown in Fig. 4. In this case, N6-SP seems to be too greedy in this aspect.

From this analysis, N4-SP raises as an interesting trade-off between the use of network bandwidth and the performance obtained while maintaining an unstructured and highly distributed policy.

3.2   A2A-SP: All-to-All Super Peer

As was shown in the previous section, increasing the amount of messages sent between super-peers improves the performance of the system. A2A-SP (all-to-all Super Peer) is the modification of the communication mechanism between super-peers in the extreme case in which every super-peer sends messages to the rest of super-peers each time. As the amount of super-peers is small compared with the total amount of nodes (2 %, 5 % or 10 % usually), this increment in the amount of control messages could prove to greatly improve the performance of the system. This topic will be covered in this section.

Figure 5 shows some promising results. In this figure, A2A-SP is compared with standard SP and Hierarchical policies in Exponential and Barabási network topologies. The difference in performance between A2A-SP and SP can be easily noted in all the cases, but is notorious in the case of 500 nodes. Moreover, an increment in the amount of super-peers does not produce a decrement in the performance of A2A-SP, while standard SP presents a strong decrement. In most of the cases, A2A-SP behaves similar to Hierarchical Policy in terms of mean GIR in both network topologies.

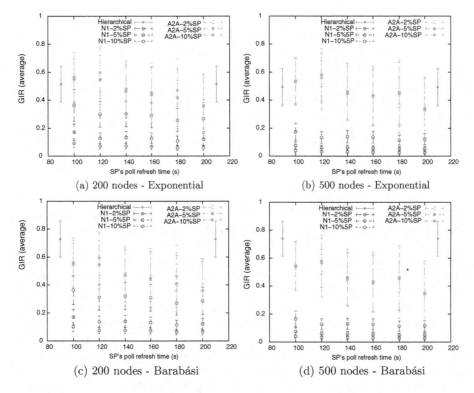

Fig. 5. Impact of variation of the refresh time in standard SP (N1-SP), Hierarchical and A2A-SP policies. Two system sizes and two network topologies are considered. The variations of A2A-SP and standard SP correspond to different amount of partitions of the system (i.e. amount of super-peers). In all the cases, A2A-SP shows better performance than standard SP. In larger systems, the difference between the two policies is even greater.

Figure 6 introduces the study of total amount of messages sent in the analyzed policies during a fixed amount of time (14 h). In the case of 200 nodes using 5 % of super-peers shown in Fig. 6(a), the amount of sent messages for A2A-SP is

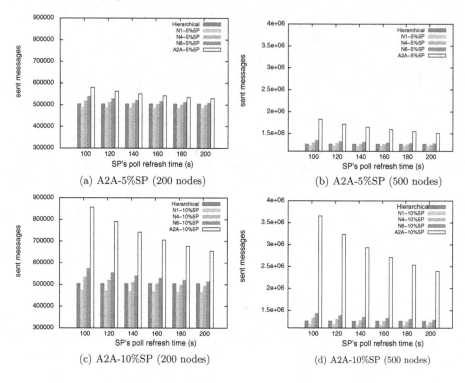

(a) A2A-5%SP (200 nodes)

(b) A2A-5%SP (500 nodes)

(c) A2A-10%SP (200 nodes)

(d) A2A-10%SP (500 nodes)

Fig. 6. Control messages sent during 14 h using Hierarchical, N1-SP, N4-SP, N6-SP and A2A-SP. In (a) and (b) 5 %SP is used, while in (c) and (d) 10 %SP. Two system sizes are considered: 200 nodes in (a) and (c), and 500 nodes in (b) and (d).

similar to other policies. The sent messages slightly increases for a larger system as can be seen in Fig. 6(b).

This situation is exacerbated when the system is further partitioned. Figure 6(c) and (d) show the amount of interchanged messages when 10 % of total nodes are super-peers (i.e. the systems is partitioned in 10 % of total nodes). In these cases, A2A-SP policy greatly exceeds the amount of messages used compared with Hierarchical and standard SP policies.

These results support that using A2A-SP policy in medium sized systems could lead to better behavior in terms of obtained GIR, maintaining the use of network in reasonable limits (i.e. comparable to Hierarchical policy). Increasing the amount of partitions in the systems produces a strong increment in the amount of messages, which could be a disadvantage of this policy in those cases.

Figure 7 presents scalability behavior for presented policies. In Fig. 7(a), N-SP is compared with standard SP and Hierarchical policy. While the system size is increased, standard SP shows a strong decay in terms of mean GIR. For the cases larger than 300 nodes, this policy turns to be almost useless. As expected, Hierarchical policy shows almost no decay in performance in the analyzed range of sizes. N-SP presents a performance which shows a slow fall with the size, but

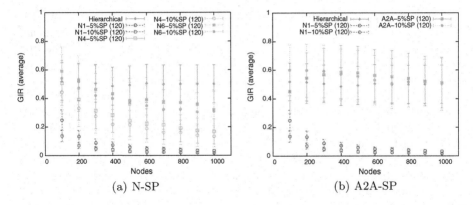

(a) N-SP   (b) A2A-SP

Fig. 7. Scalability analysis for the presented policies. Mean GIR is shown while increasing the amount of nodes in the system using fixed refresh time (120 s). Hierarchical policy is included as a reference. In Fig. (a), N-SP is compared with standard SP, while in Fig. (b) this policy is compared A2A-SP. Even though, A2A-SP presents a greater network consumption, its performance overlaps with Hierarchical. However, N4-SP and N6-SP show better performance than standard SP and rise as a trade-off in control messages interchanged and obtained performance.

overpass standard SP in all analyzed cases. N6-SP produces better results than N4-SP, none of them reaches Hierarchical policy.

Figure 7(b) shows the mean GIR for A2A-SP, standard SP and Hierarchical policies. As A2A-SP performance remains constant with the system size, it shows an excellent scalability. Even though, A2A-SP has a greater network consumption, its performance almost overlaps with Hierarchical policy.

4   Conclusions

The use of large distributed computing infrastructures has become a fundamental component in most of scientific and technological projects. Due to its highly distributed nature, one of the key topics to be addressed in large distributed systems is the determination of the availability and state of resources. Having up-to-date information of the resources in the system is extremely important to be used by the scheduler to select the appropriate target for each computational job.

There is a growing interest in the interaction with the P2P paradigm, pushing towards scalable solutions, as they share: (i) very dynamic and heterogeneous environment and (ii) creation of a virtual working environment by collecting the resources available from a series of distributed, individual entities.

Super Peer policy presents a notable improvement in terms of response time and expected number of results, compared with decentralization one. While Hierarchical policy is valuable for small and medium-sized systems, SP is more effective in very large infrastructures therefore is more scalable.

For Random policy, sending more messages each time could improve the performance of the system. Two new policies are presented changing the communication methodology between super-peers: N-SP and A2A-SP. In the first variation, a message to a randomly selected subset of the other super-peers is sent, while in A2A-SP, all the super-peers are contacted each time.

Both policies show an improvement in terms of obtained mean GIR, A2A-SP proves to get better results. Nevertheless, the network consumption of this policy could render it too expensive if the system has a high number of partitions (i.e. amount of super-peers).

As can be expected, A2A-SP presents an scalability similar to Hierarchical policy, but N-SP shows better performance than standard SP with a lower network consumption leading to a trade off between performance and used network resources.

Acknowledgments. E.M. is researcher of the CONICET. This work was partially supported by grants from Universidad de Buenos Aires (UBACyT 20020130200096BA) and CONICET (PIP 11220110100379).

References

1. Albert, R., Jeong, H., Barabási, A.L.: Internet: diameter of the world-wide web. Nature **401**, 130–131 (1999). http://adsabs.harvard.edu/abs/1999Natur.401.130A
2. Assunção, M.D., Calheiros, R.N., Bianchi, S., Netto, M.A., Buyya, R.: Big data computing and clouds: trends and future directions. J. Parallel Distrib. Comput. **79**, 3–15 (2014). http://www.sciencedirect.com/science/article/pii/S0743731514001452, Special issue on Scalable Systems for Big Data Management and Analytics
3. Barabási, A.L., Albert, R.: Emergence of scaling in random networks. Science **286**(5439), 509–512 (1999)
4. Casanova, H., Legrand, A., Quinson, M.: SimGrid: a generic framework for large-scale distributed experiments. In: 10th IEEE International Conference on Computer Modeling and Simulation, pp. 126–131. IEEE Computer Society, Los Alamitos, March 2008
5. Cesario, E., Mastroianni, C., Talia, D.: Distributed volunteer computing for solving ensemble learning problems. Future Gener. Comput. Syst. (2015, in press). http://www.sciencedirect.com/science/article/pii/S0167739X15002332
6. Ergu, D., Kou, G., Peng, Y., Shi, Y., Shi, Y.: The analytic hierarchy process: task scheduling and resource allocation in cloud computing environment. J. Supercomput. **64**(3), 835–848 (2013)
7. Foster, I., Zhao, Y., Raicu, I., Lu, S.: Cloud computing and grid computing 360-degree compared. In: 2008 Grid Computing Environments Workshop, GCE 2008, pp. 1–10, November 2008
8. Foster, I., Kesselman, C.: The Grid 2: Blueprint for a New Computing Infrastructure. The Morgan Kaufmann Series in Computer Architecture and Design. Morgan Kaufmann Publishers Inc., San Francisco (2003)
9. Foster, I., Kesselman, C., Tuecke, S.: The anatomy of the grid: enabling scalable virtual organizations. Int. J. High Perform. Comput. Appl. **15**(3), 200–222 (2001). http://portal.acm.org/citation.cfm?id=1080667

10. Ghafarian, T., Deldari, H., Javadi, B., Yaghmaee, M.H., Buyya, R.: Cycloid-grid: a proximity-aware P2P-based resource discovery architecture in volunteer computing systems. J. Future Gener. Comput. Syst. **29**(6), 1583–1595 (2013). http://www.sciencedirect.com/science/article/pii/S0167739X12001665, Including Special sections: High Performance Computing in the Cloud & Resource Discovery Mechanisms for P2P Systems
11. Iamnitchi, A., Foster, I., Nurmi, D.: A peer-to-peer approach to resource discovery in grid environments. In: Proceedings of the 11th IEEE International Symposium on High Performance Distributed Computing HPDC-11 (HPDC 2002), p. 419. IEEE, Edinbourgh, July 2002
12. Iamnitchi, A., Foster, I.: A peer-to-peer approach to resource location in Grid environments. In: Grid Resource Management: State of the Art and Future Trends, pp. 413–429. Kluwer Academic Publishers, Norwell (2004)
13. Karypis, G., Kumar, V.: A fast and high quality multilevel scheme for partitioning irregular graphs. SIAM J. Sci. Comput. **20**(1), 359–392 (1998)
14. Liu, W., Nishio, T., Shinkuma, R., Takahashi, T.: Adaptive resource discovery in mobile cloud computing. Comput. Commun. **50**, 119–129 (2014). http://www.sciencedirect.com/science/article/pii/S0140366414000590, Green Networking
15. Márquez, D.G., Mocskos, E.E., Slezak, D.F., Turjanski, P.G.: Simulation of resource monitoring and discovery in grids. In: Proceedings of HPC 2010 High-Performance Computing Symposium, pp. 3258–3270 (2010). http://www.39jaiio.org.ar/node/121
16. Mastroianni, C., Talia, D., Verta, O.: A super-peer model for resource discovery services in large-scale Grids. Future Gener. Comput. Syst. **21**(8), 1235–1248 (2005). http://www.sciencedirect.com/science/article/pii/S0167739X05000701
17. Mastroianni, C., Talia, D., Verta, O.: Designing an information system for Grids: comparing hierarchical, decentralized P2P and super-peer models. Parallel Comput. **34**(10), 593–611 (2008)
18. Mattmann, C., Garcia, J., Krka, I., Popescu, D., Medvidovic, N.: Revisiting the anatomy and physiology of the grid. J. Grid Comput. **13**(1), 19–34 (2015)
19. Mocskos, E.E., Yabo, P., Turjanski, P.G., Fernandez Slezak, D.: Grid matrix: a grid simulation tool to focus on the propagation of resource and monitoring information. Simul-T Soc. Mod. Sim. **88**(10), 1233–1246 (2012)
20. Pipan, G.: Use of the TRIPOD overlay network for resource discovery. Future Gener. Comput. Syst. **26**(8), 1257–1270 (2010). http://www.sciencedirect.com/science/article/pii/S0167739X1000018X
21. Plale, B., Jacobs, C., Jensen, S., Liu, Y., Moad, C., Parab, R., Vaidya, P.: Understanding Grid resource information management through a synthetic database benchmark/workload. In: CCGRID 2004: Proceedings of the 2004 IEEE International Symposium on Cluster Computing and the Grid, pp. 277–284. IEEE Computer Society, Washington, April 2004
22. Puppin, D., Moncelli, S., Baraglia, R., Tonellotto, N., Silvestri, F.: A grid information service based on peer-to-peer. In: Cunha, J.C., Medeiros, P.D. (eds.) Euro-Par 2005. LNCS, vol. 3648, pp. 454–464. Springer, Heidelberg (2005)
23. Ranjan, R., Harwood, A., Buyya, R.: Peer-to-peer-based resource discovery in global grids: a tutorial. IEEE Commun. Surv. Tut. **10**(2), 6–33 (2008)
24. Ranjan, R., Zhao, L.: Peer-to-peer service provisioning in cloud computing environments. J Supercomput. **65**(1), 154–184 (2013)
25. Ripeanu, M.: Peer-to-peer architecture case study: Gnutella network. In: 2001 Proceedings of the First International Conference on Peer-to-Peer Computing, pp. 99–100, August 2001

26. Shiers, J.: The worldwide LHC computing grid (worldwide LCG). Comput. Phys. Commun. **177**(1–2), 219–223 (2007)
27. Trunfio, P., Talia, D., Papadakis, C., Fragopoulou, P., Mordacchini, M., Pennanen, M., Popov, K., Vlassov, V., Haridi, S.: Peer-to-Peer resource discovery in Grids: models and systems. Future Gener. Comput. Syst. **23**(7), 864–878 (2007)
28. Williams, D.N., Drach, R., Ananthakrishnan, R., Foster, I., Fraser, D., Siebenlist, F., Bernholdt, D., Chen, M., Schwidder, J., Bharathi, S., et al.: The earth system grid: enabling access to multimodel climate simulation data. Bull. Am. Meteorol. Soc. **90**(2), 195–205 (2009)

GPU and MIC Computing: Methods, Libraries and Applications

Asynchronous in Situ Processing with Gromacs: Taking Advantage of GPUs

Monica L. Hernandez[1,2]([✉]), Matthieu Dreher[2,3],
Carlos J. Barrios[1], and Bruno Raffin[2]

[1] Universidad Industrial de Santander, Bucaramanga, Colombia
monica.hernandez2@correo.uis.edu.co
[2] INRIA, University Grenoble Alpes, Montbonnot-Saint-Martin, France
[3] Argonne National Laboratory, Lemont, USA

Abstract. Numerical simulations using supercomputers are producing an ever growing amount of data. Efficient production and analysis of these data are the key to future discoveries. The in situ paradigm is emerging as a promising solution to avoid the I/O bottleneck encountered in the file system for both the simulation and the analytics by treating the data as soon as they are produced in memory. Various strategies and implementations have been proposed in the last years to support in situ treatments with a low impact on the simulation performance. Yet, little efforts have been made when it comes to perform in situ analytics with hybrid simulations supporting accelerators like GPUs. In this article, we propose a study of the in situ strategies with Gromacs, a molecular dynamic simulation code supporting multi-GPUs, as our application target. We specifically focus on the computational resources usage of the machine by the simulation and the in situ analytics. We finally extend the usual in situ placement strategies to the case of in situ analytics running on a GPU and study their impact on both Gromacs performance and the resource usage of the machine. We show in particular that running in situ analytics on the GPU can be a more efficient solution than on the CPU especially when the CPU is the bottleneck of the simulation.

Keywords: In situ analysis · FlowVR · Graphics Processing Units · Gromacs

1 Introduction

Large scale simulations are an important tool for scientists in various domains such as biology, fluid dynamic, material science or astrophysics. Yet, it is becoming more and more challenging to analyze the ever growing amount of data produced by these simulations. In 2010 already, a turbulence simulation (GTC [13]) was producing 260 GB of data every 2 min using only 16384 cores [33]. More recently, in biology, the complete atomistic model of the HIV capsid has been determined [32]. Several simulations, each producing about 50 TB of data for a total of 1 PB, were required to build this model.

© Springer International Publishing Switzerland 2015
C. Osthoff et al. (Eds.): CARLA 2015, CCIS 565, pp. 89–106, 2015.
DOI: 10.1007/978-3-319-26928-3_7

In the Exascale era, it is estimated that less than 1 % of the data produced by simulation will be saved because of bandwidth constraints [19]. Writing raw data to disks will no longer be viable because of the resulting loss of information.

The in situ paradigm is emerging as one promising solution to this problem. The principle is to process data as close as possible to their source while data still reside in memory [31]. Both the simulation and analytics benefit from this approach since they do not have to write/read to/from the file system. Although this approach was initially designed for I/O, numerous applications are possible: live visualization, statistics generation, feature tracking, simulation monitoring, etc. However, setting up such analysis can be challenging. As both simulation and analysis run concurrently, contention for the computational and network resources can lead to significant degradations of the simulation performance. Several strategies and systems have been proposed to mitigate this penalty in the last few years.

Another benefit from in situ processing is to improve the global resource usage of the machine. Usually, simulation codes cannot fully use and scale with all the computational resources available on large parallel machines [35]. For instance, running the GTS code on 512 cores using only 3 out of 4 cores per socket reduces the simulation performances by only 2.7 % compare to using all the available cores [36]. For these cases, it can be more efficient to use the fourth core to run in situ analytics to accelerate the analysis phase and therefore shorten the time to discovery.

Efficiently using hybrid computational resources such as CPUs and accelerators is even more challenging for simulation codes. In the last years, various leadership parallel machines such as Tianhe-2 or BlueWaters have integrated accelerators (GPUs, Xeon PHI). The future 150+ petaflop machine Summit at Oak Ridge National Laboratory will also integrate GPUs in its architecture. These accelerators offer a high Flops/Watt ratio that is required to reach Exascale. Several codes such as NAMD [20] or Gromacs [11] have been adapted to benefit from these accelerators and lead to significant speedups.Yet, in most cases, not all the computations are performed on the accelerator. Consequently, there are some periods during the simulation execution where the accelerator is idle leading to underused resources.

Significant efforts have been made by the community to propose in situ systems with a low impact on the simulation performance. Yet, most of them focused on simulations and analytics running only on CPUs [5,7,29,35]. In this article, we study current in situ strategies applied to hybrid simulations. Gromacs, a well established molecular dynamics simulation package supporting multi-GPUs, is our application target. We first study the usage of the computational resources by Gromacs native during classical runs. Then we study the resource usage when in situ analytics are running on the CPU using asynchronous time-partitioning and helper core strategies. We rely on FlowVR [3,7], a middleware for asynchronous in situ/in transit applications, to implement these strategies. Finally, we adapt these two strategies for in situ analytics running on GPUs and analyze the resource usage. We show in particular that running in situ analytics on the

GPU can be a more efficient solution than on the CPU especially when the CPU is the bottleneck of the simulation.

The rest of the article is organized as follow: we first discuss the related work (Sect. 2); then, we present Gromacs and the framework used to perform our experiments (Sect. 3). We present our experimental results (Sect. 4) and summarize our findings (Sect. 5).

2   Related Work

In this section, we first present the systems and strategies to perform in situ treatments. Then we present some use cases of treatments with GPUs in the context of in situ or off-line processing.

2.1   In Situ Systems

One key design decision for in situ systems is the placement of analytics processing.

The most direct approach is to host the simulation and the analytics on the same computational resources. This strategy, called time-partitioning, is usually the easiest to implement. It can also enable the simulation and the analytics to share data structures leading to a reduced memory footprint. Ma et al. [31] integrated a volume rendering engine directly into the code of a turbulence simulation. About 10 % of the total execution time is spent in the rendering step. Common visualization tools like Visit [30] or Paraview [9] have lightweight libraries to instrument the simulation. Their main purpose is to convert the simulation data format to the VTK format before executing an analysis pipeline. Tu et al. [28] propose a fully integrated solution with an earthquake simulation and the Hercules framework to perform in situ visualization. The only output is a set of JPEG images. For these systems, the time spent running the analytics is directly added to the simulation time. This approach can be very costly in both time and memory. A study has been proposed with Catalyst [18] on industrial simulations. With commonly used analysis scenarios, they observed up to 30 % of increased execution time and up to 300 % increased memory consumption because of data conversion requirements. Goldrush [35] tackles the problem of the global execution time by making the treatments asynchronous. To limit the impact of the asynchronous treatments on the simulation run time, the treatments are scheduled when the simulation is not using all the available cores (outside of an OpenMP section).The goal is to improve the global resource usage of the machine by scheduling the analysis when the resources are underused.

Other works propose dedicated resources to perform in situ analytics. This approach, called space-partitioning, allows asynchronous in situ analytics execution, avoids some contention on the computational resource but requires at least one data copy. Some systems, like Damaris [5], use dedicated cores (called *helper cores*) on each simulation node to execute asynchronously the in situ analytics. Data are copied from the simulation into a shared-memory space. Analytics can then read and process data from this space asynchronously. Applications such as I/O or scientific visualization with Visit [6] are then possible. The *helper core* strategy has also been used by Functional Partitioning [16] and GePSeA [22] mainly to focus on I/O operations.

Other systems propose to use a separate set of nodes (called *staging nodes*) to execute analytics (called in transit analytics). PreData [33] is built within the ADIOS framework [17] and allows to execute lightweight in situ operations before moving the data to *staging nodes*. Data are then processed in transit using a Map/Reduce like model. DataTap is used to schedule the data transfer when the simulation is in a computation phase and is not using the network card extensively. HDF5/DMS [23] uses the HDF5 interface to capture the data and store them in a distributed shared memory space. Other applications can then read the data with the read HDF5 API usually on a different set of nodes. DataSpaces [4] implements a distributed publish/subscribe system. The simulation pushes data in a indexed distributed space and other treatments retrieve the necessary data.

More recently, hybrid systems combining both in situ (synchronous or not) and in transit treatments have emerged. Fheng et al. [34] highlight the necessity of placement flexibility of analytics and propose an analytical model to evaluate the cost of the placement strategies. Glean [29] allows synchronous in situ treatments and asynchronous in transit treatments. FlexIO [36] is built on top of ADIOS and allows asynchronous in situ treatments on dedicated cores and asynchronous in transit treatments.The system monitors the performance of the simulation and can migrate the analytics at runtime or slow them down if they are impacting too much the simulation performance. FlowVR [3,7] allows describing a data-flow between components (simulation, analysis modules). Treatments are performed asynchronously from the simulation. The user can specify the location of the treatments: on a set of helper cores, staging nodes, or on the same resources as the simulation.

Our work in this paper follows the work done on helper core approaches and asynchronous time-partitioning approaches. We extend these works to the domain of multi-GPU simulations and in situ analytics using GPUs. To implement our approach, we rely on the FlowVR middleware to host and coordinate the in situ analytics execution.

2.2   Treatments with GPU

An implementation of in situ systems using GPUs is the work presented by R. Hagan et al. [10] who propose a load balancing method for in situ visualization in a multiGPU system. This method is based on an asynchronous space sharing strategy where $N/2$ GPUs are used as dedicated GPUs for visualization, N being the number of GPUs in the system. The other $N/2$ GPUs perform the N-body simulation and transfer the data processed to RAM. Once in the memory, the data are transferred to the dedicated GPU to perform rendering task through a ray tracing visualization algorithm. Each GPU is managed with separate buffers on the CPU side in order to write/read the data to/from memory asynchronously.

Performing off-line processing on GPUs is a growing field of interest. VMD [12] is a widely used tool for visualization and analysis of biological systems such as proteins and nucleic acids. Over the last years, many visualizations and analytics have been adapted to support GPUs using CUDA. The Quicksurf algorithm [14], for instance, has been proposed to visualize molecular surfaces of large ensembles of atoms. It has been recently used to visualize the full model of the HIV capsid on BlueWaters [27]. Other analysis such as radial distribution functions [15], fitting [26] and many others [24] are accelerated with GPUs. Although VMD does not have a full support for in situ analysis, some interactive applications combining simulation and live visualization are possible such as Interactive Molecular Dynamic simulations [25].

3   Framework Description

3.1   Gromacs

We describe here the features of Gromacs that are needed to understand its behavior and performance. The reader can refer to [11,21] for complementary details.

Gromacs is a commonly used parallel molecular dynamics simulation package. It is able to scale to several millions of atoms on several thousands of cores by using MPI, OpenMP, and CUDA. The internal organization of Gromacs is a master/slave approach. The master process is responsible for maintaining a global state when necessary and performing the I/O operations.

Atoms are distributed in a irregular grid where each cell of the grid is managed by one MPI process. We call *home atoms* of an MPI process the atoms belonging to its cell. The cell sizes of the grid are adjusted at runtime by a dynamic load-balancing system. The main computation part is that of the forces: bonded interactions between atoms sharing a link and non-bonded interactions for the distant atoms. Non-bonded interactions are the most computationally expensive operations because they require N-to-N communications. Performance timings are monitored during this phase to load-balance the simulation.

Since version 4.6, Gromacs supports GPUs with CUDA, where no bond interactions are transferred to the GPUs while the bonded-interactions are executed in parallel on the CPU. Gromacs also supports multi-GPUs: each GPU is assigned to an MPI process; OpenMP is used to fill the rest of the cores when more cores than GPUs are available on a node. Since the bonded and non-bonded computations are performed concurrently, a balance must be found between CPU and GPU computations. The dynamic load-balancing system monitors the difference of computation time between the CPU and the GPU and adjusts the grid dimensions accordingly.

3.2   FlowVR

FlowVR [7] is our middleware to create asynchronous in situ applications. It allows describing an application as a graph, where nodes are data operations and edges are communication channels. A node is called a module and is equipped with input and output ports. A module runs an infinite loop. At each iteration, a module can receive data, process them, and send computed data to the rest of the application. The loop is implemented with three main functions: *wait, get*, and *put*. *Wait* blocks the module until there is at least one message in all input ports. *Get* returns the oldest message from an input port's queue. *Put* sends a message to an output port. Both *Get* and *Put* functions are nonblocking.

A module has no knowledge of the data source and destination. The data channels are described in a Python script that declares the global application and creates the links between the modules. Each module is assigned to a host and possibly to a set of cores on the host. A daemon is hosted on each node in the application. It hosts a shared memory segment in which the modules are reading and writing their data. If two modules are on the same host, the daemon does a simple exchange of pointers in the shared memory space. Otherwise, the local daemon sends the message to the daemon hosting the remote module, which will write the data in its shared memory space and pass the pointer to its module.

FlowVR does not impose any restrictions on the resources used by a module. Any module is free to use OpenMP or GPUs to accelerate its treatment. However, FlowVR does not provide any protections in case several modules are using intensively the same resources.

For more details, the reader can refer to [7].

3.3   Gromacs-FlowVR Interaction

We have instrumented the simulation code Gromacs with a similar method than our previous works [7,8]. For each MPI process, we declare one module with one output port to extract the atom positions. This approach allows us to preserve the same level of parallelism of the data, which can be used later by in situ analytics.

We modified the main loop of Gromacs to periodically extract the atom positions. Every x iterations, with x a user-defined parameter, each module performs a FlowVR *wait()*, copies the positions of the *home atoms* inside a FlowVR message, and puts the message. The atom positions are then sent to the rest of the application, if the output ports of the modules are connected to other modules such as in situ analytics. Otherwise, the data are erased because they are not used anymore by any module. Note that because the Gromacs modules do not have any input ports, the *wait()* will return immediately and not block the simulation. In order to minimize any noise in the simulation performance, we have also disabled the native writing system of Gromacs.

3.4   Benchmark Framework Description

We implemented a framework to perform in situ analytics based on two different placement strategies: *helper core* and *overlapping*. For all strategies, the simulation and the in situ analytics have the possibility to use GPUs.

The *helper core* strategy reserves one core per node to perform in situ analytics (see Fig. 1(a)). Data are gathered on each node asynchronously and sent to one or several in situ tasks hosted on the helper core. We assigned one GPU per simulation process and one GPU for the analytics.

The *overlapping* strategy runs on the same resources as the simulation (see Fig. 1(b)). In our case, we instantiated as many in situ tasks as there are MPI processes per node. Therefore, each MPI process of the simulation sends the data to the in situ task located on the same core as the MPI process. Note that the in situ tasks are running asynchronously with the simulation. Each GPU is shared between one simulation process and one in situ task. At runtime, both simulation and analytics kernels run concurrently on each GPU.

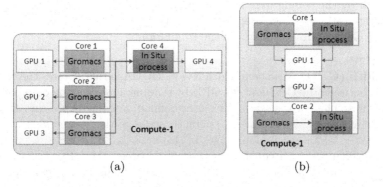

(a)   (b)

Fig. 1. (a) Helper core strategy. A dedicated core is allocated for in situ analytics. Data are gathered by the node and sent asynchronously to the in situ tasks (b) overlapping strategy. One in situ task is instantiated for each MPI process of the simulation.

The in situ analytics are triggered each time the simulation outputs data. The different analytics used are described in the next section. In these two particular setups, the communication channels are simple FIFO channels between the simulation and analytics modules. Overflows can occur if the analytics do not follow the pace of the simulation. For this framework, this is an acceptable situation since the data produced are relatively small and just a few output steps are performed. For real application scenarios, special components can be added to sample the output data from the simulation. It is also possible to block the simulation at the next output step if the previous output step has not been analyzed yet.

3.5   Benchmarks

We designed this framework to evaluate the impact of in situ CPU/GPU tasks on Gromacs performance and the resource usage of the machine. We adopted the same approach as in [35]. We implemented several micro benchmarks, each designed to stress specific parts of a multi-GPU parallel machine. Each of these benchmarks is available for *overlapping* and *helper core* strategies.

PI (CPU). The PI benchmark, used by Zheng et al. in [35], stresses the floating point units of the processors. When PI is triggered, x iterations, with x an user-defined parameter, are performed to estimate the value of π. For both strategies, *overlapping* and *helper core*, we execute the same total number of PI iterations. With the *helper core* strategy, only one in situ process computes all the iterations (x). In the case of the *overlapping* strategy, N in situ processes are used. The x iterations are then distributed evenly among all the in situ tasks (x/N).

This benchmark perturbs the CPU while both the CPU and GPU are intensively used by the simulation. The simulation load-balances both the CPU and GPU computations. Therefore, perturbing the CPU should impact both the CPU and GPU computations from the simulation.

Bandwidth (GPU). The bandwidth Nvidia CUDA kernel stresses the communications between the CPU and the GPU by sending and receiving data packages several times. The message sizes s are user-defined. For the *helper core* strategy, one GPU receives messages of size s. In the case of the *overlapping* strategy, each of the N GPUs receives messages of size s/N.

Data exchanges are frequently performed between the CPU and the GPU during the simulation. Perturbing the GPU data transmission can delay the GPU computations of the simulation waiting for their data transfers.

Matrix Multiplication (GPU). The multMatrix Nvidia CUDA kernel is a compute-intensive kernel multiplying 2 matrices several times. The sizes of the two matrices are 640×320 and 320×320, respectively. The number of multiplications y performed during one iteration of the benchmark is user defined. With the *helper core* strategy, one in situ process does all the matrix multiplications (y). In the case of the *overlapping* strategy, N in situ processes performed y/N.

This benchmark occupies the processing units of the GPU. The kernels of the simulation will have less multiprocessors available to be scheduled leading to delays of the simulation computations.

The impact of the benchmarks on the simulation performance depends not only on the benchmark but also on the balance of GPU/CPU computations adopted by the simulation. If the CPU is the limiting factor of the simulation, the GPU benchmark should be less damaging and vice versa if the GPU is the limiting factor.

4 Experiments

4.1 Experimental Context

We ran our experiments on the cluster *GUANE-1 (GpUs Advanced eNviromEnt)* at *Universidad Industrial de Santander*. Each node is a 8-core Intel® Xeon® CPU E5640 @ 2.67 GHz (two sockets with 4 cores each one) with hyper-threading activated (16 logical cores), 103 GB of RAM and 8 Nvidia Tesla M2050 GPUs (448 cores each). Interprocess communication is done through a 1 GB Ethernet network. For all experiments, Gromacs runs a Martini simulation (simulation of atom aggregates) with a patch of 54000 lipids representing about 2.1 million particles in coarse grain [1]. Gromacs is very sensitive to the quality of the network due to its high frequency [2]. Therefore, we preferred to avoid intranode communications and used only one node for our experiments. For all experiments, the native writing method of Gromacs is disabled.

We measured both the simulation performance and the GPU utilization for each experiment. The performance metric is iterations per second (higher is better). Each simulation lasted at least 1000 iteration steps to avoid performance jittering due to the dynamic load-balancing at the initialization phase. The GPU utilization is measured with the tool nvidia-smi[1] from Nvidia. The GPU utilization indicates the percent of time over the past second during which one or more kernel were executed on each GPU. We took the highest GPU utilization that we found from every experiment (five measures with nvidia-smi per experiment).

4.2 Gromacs Native

We first benchmarked Gromacs stand alone (no code modification) to determine which configuration (number of threads, MPI processes, GPUs) provides the best performance on our node.

Figure 2 presents the results for Gromacs running on the CPU only and in hybrid mode using GPUs. As a reminder we use 1 GPU for each MPI process. For both cases, we used 2 OpenMP threads per MPI process with the 2 threads mapped to the same physical core (hyperthreading). The hybrid version outperforms the CPU version in all cases by a factor from 3.2 for 8 MPI processes to 4.38 for 2 MPI processes.

---

[1] https://developer.nvidia.com/nvidia-system-management-interface.

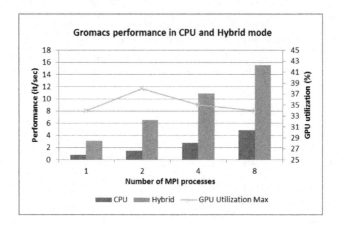

Fig. 2. Native Gromacs performance and GPU utilization when increasing the number of MPI process

During the simulation, CPU and GPU computations are performed concurrently. The computations are balanced at runtime by Gromacs. According to Gromacs internal logs, for each hybrid configuration, the CPU is not waiting for the GPU. This can indicate that the GPU is idle while the CPU completes its computation.

The GPU utilization of Fig. 2 indicates the maximum percentage of time where at least one CUDA kernel is active. In the best case, for 2 MPI processes, the GPU is used at most only 38 % of the time. Moreover, when the simulation kernels are running, the GPU occupancy is only of 60 %[2].

Although Gromacs greatly benefits from using multiple GPUs, these resources are underused by the simulation. These results indicate that, in the case of Gromacs, the CPU is the limiting factor in the computation.

4.3   Gromacs Instrumented with FlowVR

We measured the performances of both the native Gromacs and our FlowVR-instrumented version. For each MPI process, we allocate 2 OpenMP threads and 1 GPU as previously. For the FlowVR-instrumented version, we extracted the data every 100 simulation iterations.

At most, our instrumentation cost increases the simulation time by 0.5 % in the case of 2 MPI processes. The impact on the GPU utilization is also negligible. These results demonstrate that our instrumentation method does not impact the simulation behavior. This cost is significantly lower than our previous report [7]. This is explained by a much lower output frequency. Previously, we extracted data every 10 ms. For this study, we only extract the data every 6 seconds. As the instrumentation blocks the simulation for about 0.2 ms at each output step (*Wait()* and copy of the atom positions), the cost of instrumentation is negligible

---

[2] Measured with nvprof.

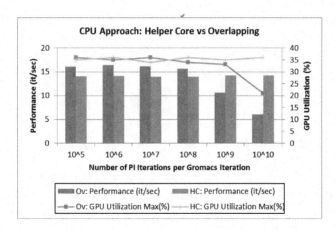

Fig. 3. Helper core (HC) and overlapping (Ov) strategies when increasing the number of PI iterations performed per Gromacs iteration.

4.4 Gromacs with CPU Analytics

We measured the performances of Gromacs while running asynchronous in situ analytics on the CPU. We used the PI benchmark described in Sect. 3.5 in both *helper core* and *overlapping* strategies. Gromacs outputs data every 100 simulation iterations. For each Gromacs output, we triggered y iterations of PI in total. Figure 3 shows the simulation performance and GPU utilization for both strategies while varying y.

The *overlapping* strategy gives the best performance as long as the extra computations are not intense. For less than 10^8 PI iterations, the simulation is slowed by less than 4 % while the GPU utilization stays at the same level as Gromacs native. However, for a larger number of PI iterations, the simulation performance is dropping as y is increasing. For 10^9 iterations, the performance degradation is higher than 30 % while the GPU utilization drops by 3 %. For 10^{10} iterations, the degradation of both simulation performance and GPU utilization is even higher.

The *helper core* strategy displays a more stable behavior. The initial cost with a low number of PI iterations is higher than the *overlapping* strategy. This is expected since one core and one GPU are removed from the simulation resources. However, as the in situ tasks are not hosted on the same resources as the simulation, the increasing computational charge is not affecting the simulation performance. Figure 3 shows that between 10^8 and 10^9 iteration, the *helper core* strategy becomes more efficient than the *overlapping* strategy.

The GPU utilization is reduced by the in situ analytics although the PI benchmark does not use the GPU. For the *helper Core* strategy, 1 GPU is not being used during all the simulation whereas for *overlapping*, the GPU utilization is lower than 36 % for all the tests. Gromacs balances its computations between

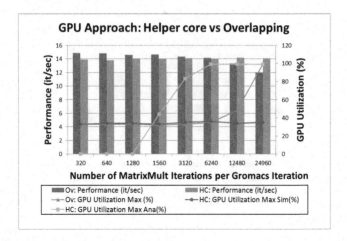

Fig. 4. Helper core (HC) and overlapping (Ov) strategies when increasing the number y of matrix multiplications perform per Gromacs Iteration. The GPU utilization for helper core strategy is split in two curves. GPU Utilization Max Sim indicates the maximum utilization of the 7 GPUs used by the simulation. GPU Utilization Max Ana is the GPU utilization for the GPU used by the in situ multMatrix.

the CPU and GPU. However, previous results (Sect. 4.2) showed that the CPU is the bottleneck of the simulation. As the PI benchmark stresses the CPU, Gromacs requires more time to launch the GPU kernels, leading to more idle time on the GPU with the *overlapping* strategy.

In summary, traditional in situ analytics running on the CPU fail to improve the global resource usage of Gromacs in hybrid mode. With the *helper core* strategy, one GPU is not used. With the *overlapping* strategy, the bottleneck of the simulation is more stressed by the analytics leading to more idle time on the GPUs. Others strategies are necessary to improve the global usage of resource.

4.5   Gromacs with GPU Analytics

Rather than stressing the CPU, which is already the bottleneck of our simulation, we propose to perform in situ analytics on the GPU. We first used the multMatrix benchmark described in Sect. 3.5. As previously, Gromacs outputs data every 100 iterations. For each Gromacs output, y matrix multiplications are performed in total.

Figure 4 shows the simulation performance and GPU utilization for both strategies. As for the CPU benchmark, the *overlapping* strategy is more efficient for light computations. For less than $y = 3120$ matrix multiplications per Gromacs output, the simulation frequency is reduced by less than 12 %, while the GPU utilization stays at the same level as Gromacs native. However, for larger numbers of multiplications, the performance drops up to 20 %, but the GPU utilization is increasing up to 99 %.

The *helper core* strategy (referred as HC), displays stable behavior like the CPU benchmark. The initial cost with a low number of matrix multiplications is higher than the *overlapping* strategy. Because the in situ tasks are not hosted on the same resources as the simulation, however the increasing computational charge is not affecting the simulation performance further. Figure 4 shows that between 6,240 and 12,480 matrix multiplications, the *helper GPU* strategy keeps a fixed cost and outperforms the *overlapping* strategy. This strategy also allows the GPU utilization to increase up to 99 %.

We observe the following general trends. First, *overlapping* and *helper core* have similar behavior with CPU and GPU in situ analytics. The *overlapping* cost increases with a growing number of in situ computations. The *helper core* strategy has a higher initial cost for a small number of multiplications but does not further impact the simulation performance for higher computational cost. Secondly, performing in situ analytics on the GPU improves the GPU utilization. Because the simulation does not fully use the GPUs, other kernels can be launched with a limited impact on the simulation performance.

The multMatrix benchmark performs computations but does not transfer data between the CPU and GPU. Only the computational units are stressed. However, when performing data intensive analytics, data transfers must also be considered.

On our nodes, the 8 GPUs are connected to 3 PCI express ports. They share the same bus to transfer data from/to the GPU. We used the Bandwidth benchmark described in Sect. 3.5 to evaluate the impact of intensive in situ data analytics on the simulation performance. As previously, Gromacs outputs data every 100 iterations. For each Gromacs output, five rounds of data transfers are performed each with a given message size.

Figure 5 shows the simulation performance for both strategies. For this benchmark, we do not indicate the GPU utilization since the benchmark does not use the GPU. The *overlapping* strategy's impact on the simulation performance is

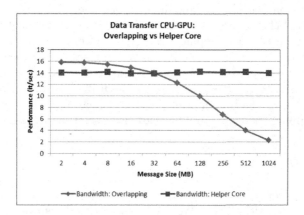

Fig. 5. Helper core and overlapping strategies when increasing the size of the message transferred.

less noticeable when the size of the message transferred is smaller than 32 MB. However, for a bigger message size, the performance drops up to 85 % for message sizes of 1GB. The *helper core* strategy preserves a good isolation between the simulation and the in situ analytics and keeps a fixed cost. Two factors can explain this result. First, our GPUs are connected in a 3-3-2 pattern on the PCI express buses. We placed the dedicated GPU on the third bus which only hosts 2 GPUs. Therefore, the in situ analytics only disturb one GPU of the simulation on the bus which is the less stressed. Secondly, molecular dynamics codes are not data-intensive codes. The full molecular model represents only a few MB of data to transfer to/from the GPU. This leaves room on the buses to transfer data for other tasks.

4.6   Discussion

With these experiments, we have shown that we can apply the same placement strategies for GPU in situ analytics as for CPU strategies and observe similar behaviors. Moreover, in the case of Gromacs, using the GPUs for in situ analytics improves the GPU utilization while keeping a cost similar to the CPU strategies. This is possible for two reasons. First, the bottleneck of Gromacs is the CPU in our setup. This leaves more room on the GPU than on the CPU. Second, Gromacs is not a data-intensive application which makes it less sensitive to other data transfer.

Our goal in this article is to show that, in the case of hybrid simulations, there is also a need for placement flexibility to compute in situ analytics. For a pure CPU simulation, the placement strategy generally depends on the cost of the computation and the nature of the analytics. However, for a hybrid simulation, the balance of CPU/GPU computation is another parameter to take into account. Depending of whether the CPU or the GPU is the simulation bottleneck, in situ analytics should be performed on the less loaded resource if possible.

The simulation setup presented here leaves the GPUs idle a significant amount of time. This allows us to schedule heavy computational in situ tasks on the GPUs with the Overlapping strategy for a limited cost. However, other types of simulation might use the GPUs more intensively. For such scenarios, it is likely that for the same computational in situ tasks, the helper core strategy becomes more efficient. We expect that, as the utilization of the GPUs by the simulation increases, the computational charge manageable at a reasonable cost by the Overlapping strategy would decrease in favor of the Helper core strategy.

5   Conclusion

We presented a study of the impact of in situ analytics in the case of the Gromacs simulation running with GPUs. We first showed that Gromacs is not natively able to fully use the available GPUs leading to underused resources. Then we showed that common in situ placement strategies such as using a dedicated core or asynchronous time-partitioning can amplify this phenomenon in the case of Gromacs. As an alternative approach, we used the GPUs to process analytics and applied the same placement strategies as for the CPU in situ analytics. CPU and GPU in situ analytics impact the simulation performance in a similar way with the same placement strategy. However, GPU analytics improve the global GPU utilization. We showed that, when considering hybrid simulation using GPUs, the balance between CPU and GPU computation should be taken into account when selecting a placement strategy for in situ analytics.

Our future work will focus on building real-case applications combining an hybrid simulation with hybrid in situ analytics. Tools such as VMD are available to perform analytics on the GPU. We will also extend this study to the case of In-Transit analytics. Some supercomputers such as *BlueWaters* have hybrid architectures combining CPU nodes and GPU nodes that can bring new trade-offs in the analytics placement. We will also study the recent feature in GPUs with compute capability 4.0 to launch CUDA kernels with a priority level. This feature can bring new opportunities especially for *Overlapping* strategies to perform in situ analytics at a lower priority than the simulation.

Acknowledgments. Experiments presented in this paper were carried out using the GridUIS-2 experimental testbed, being developed under the Universidad Industrial de Santander (SC3UIS) High Performance and Scientific Computing Centre, development action with support from UIS Vicerrectoria de Investigacin y Extension (VIE-UIS) and several UIS research groups as well as other funding bodies (http://www.sc3.uis.edu.co).

References

1. http://philipwfowler.wordpress.com/2013/10/23/gromacs-4-6-scaling-of-a-very-large-coarse-grained-system/
2. http://www.hpcadvisorycouncil.com/pdf/GROMACS_Analysis_AMD.pdf
3. Allard, J., Gouranton, V., Lecointre, L., Limet, S., Melin, E., Raffin, B., Robert, S.: FlowVR: a middleware for large scale virtual reality applications. In: Proceedings of Euro-Par 2004, Pisa, Italia (August 2004)
4. Docan, C., Parashar, M., Klasky, S.: DataSpaces: an interaction and coordination framework for coupled simulation workflows. Cluster Comput. **15**, 163–181 (2012)
5. Dorier, M., Antoniu, G., Cappello, F., Snir, M., Orf, L.: Damaris: how to efficiently leverage multicore parallelism to achieve scalable, Jitter-Free I/O. In: CLUSTER - IEEE International Conference on Cluster Computing. IEEE, September 2012
6. Dorier, M., Sisneros, Roberto, R., Peterka, T., Antoniu, G., Semeraro, Dave, B.: Damaris/Viz: a nonintrusive, adaptable and user-friendly in situ visualization framework. In: LDAV - IEEE Symposium on Large-Scale Data Analysis and Visualization, Atlanta, United States, October 2013
7. Dreher, M., Raffin, B.: A flexible framework for asynchronous in situ and in transit analytics for scientific simulations. In: 2014 14th IEEE/ACM International Symposium on Cluster, Cloud and Grid Computing (CCGrid), May 2014

8. Dreher, M., Piuzzi, M., Ahmed, T., Matthieu, C., Baaden, M., Férey, N., Limet, S., Raffin, B., Robert, S.: Interactive molecular dynamics: scaling up to large systems. In: International Conference on Computational Science, ICCS 2013. Elsevier, Barcelone, Spain, June 2013

9. Fabian, N., Moreland, K., Thompson, D., Bauer, A., Marion, P., Geveci, B., Rasquin, M., Jansen, K.: The paraview coprocessing library: a scalable, general purpose in situ visualization library. In: 2011 IEEE Symposium on Large Data Analysis and Visualization (LDAV), October 2011

10. Hagan, R., Cao, Y.: Multi-GPU load balancing for in-situ visualization. In: The 2011 International Conference on Parallel and Distributed Processing Techniques and Applications (2011)

11. Hess, B., Kutzner, C., van der Spoel, D., Lindahl, E.: GROMACS 4: algorithms for highly efficient, load-balanced, and scalable molecular simulation. J. Chem. Theory Comput. **4**, 435–447 (2008)

12. Humphrey, W., Dalke, A., Schulten, K.: VMD - visual molecular dynamics. J. Mol. Graph. **14**, 33–38 (1996)

13. Klasky, S., Ethier, S., Lin, Z., Martins, K., Mccune, D., Samtaney, R.: Grid-based parallel data streaming implemented for the Gyrokinetic Toroidal code. In: Supercomputing Conference (SC 2003). IEEE Computer Society (2003)

14. Krone, M., Stone, J.E., Ertl, T., Schulten, K.: Fast visualization of Gaussian density surfaces for molecular dynamics and particle system trajectories. In: EuroVis 2012 Short Papers, vol. 1 (2012)

15. Levine, B.G., Stone, J.E., Kohlmeyer, A.: Fast analysis of molecular dynamics trajectories with graphics processing units Radial distribution function histogramming. J. Comput. Phys. **230**(9), 3556–3569 (2011)

16. Li, M., Vazhkudai, S.S., Butt, A.R., Meng, F., Ma, X., Kim, Y., Engelmann, C., Shipman, G.: Functional partitioning to optimize end-to-end performance on many-core architectures. In: Proceedings of the 2010 ACM/IEEE International Conference for High Performance Computing, Networking, Storage and Analysis, SC 2010. IEEE Computer Society, Washington (2010)

17. Lofstead, J.F., Klasky, S., Schwan, K., Podhorszki, N., Jin, C.: Flexible IO and integration for scientific codes through the adaptable IO system (ADIOS). In: 6th International Workshop on Challenges of Large Applications in Distributed Environments (2008)

18. Lorendeau, B., Fournier, Y., Ribes, A.: In-situ visualization in fluid mechanics using catalyst: a case study for code saturne. In: 2013 IEEE Symposium on Large-Scale Data Analysis and Visualization (LDAV), October 2013

19. Moreland, K.: Oh, $#! Exascale! the effect of emerging architectures on scientific discovery. In: High Performance Computing, Networking, Storage and Analysis (SCC), 2012 SC Companion, November 2012

20. Phillips, J.C., Braun, R., Wang, W., Gumbart, J., Tajkhorshid, E., Villa, E., Chipot, C., Skeel, R.D., Kal, L., Schulten, K.: Scalable molecular dynamics with NAMD. J. Comput. Chem. **26**(16), 1781–1802 (2005)

21. Pronk, S., Pall, S., Schulz, R., Larsson, P., Bjelkmar, P., Apostolov, R., Shirts, M.R., Smith, J.C., Kasson, P.M., van der Spoel, D., Hess, B., Lindahl, E.: Gromacs 4.5: a high-throughput and highly parallel open source molecular simulation toolkit. Bioinformatics (2013)

22. Singh, A., Balaji, P., Feng, W.c.: GePSeA: a general-purpose software acceleration framework for lightweight task offloading. In: Proceedings of the 2009 International Conference on Parallel Processing, ICPP 2009. IEEE Computer Society, Washington (2009)

23. Soumagne, J., Biddiscombe, J.: Computational steering and parallel online monitoring using RMA through the HDF5 DSM virtual file driver. In: Proceedings of the International Conference on Computational Science, ICCS 2011, Singapore, vol. 4, June 2011

24. Stone, J.E., Hardy, D.J., Ufimtsev, I.S., Schulten, K.: GPU-accelerated molecular modeling coming of age. J. Mol. Graph. Model. 29(2), 116–125 (2010)

25. Stone, J.E., Kohlmeyer, A., Vandivort, K.L., Schulten, K.: Immersive molecular visualization and interactive modeling with commodity hardware. In: Bebis, G., et al. (eds.) ISVC 2010, Part II. LNCS, vol. 6454, pp. 382–393. Springer, Heidelberg (2010)

26. Stone, J.E., McGreevy, R., Isralewitz, B., Schulten, K.: GPU accelerated analysis and visualization of large structures solved by molecular dynamics flexible fitting. Faraday discussions 169 (2014)

27. Stone, J.E., Vandivort, K.L., Schulten, K.: GPU-accelerated molecular visualization on petascale supercomputing platforms. In: Proceedings of the 8th International Workshop on Ultrascale Visualization, UltraVis 2013. ACM, New York (2013)

28. Tu, T., Yu, H., Ramirez-Guzman, L., Bielak, J., Ghattas, O., Ma, K.L., O'Hallaron, D.: From mesh generation to scientific visualization: an end-to-end approach to parallel supercomputing. In: SC 2006 Conference, Proceedings of the ACM/IEEE, November 2006

29. Vishwanath, V., Hereld, M., Papka, M.: Toward simulation-time data analysis and I/O acceleration on leadership-class systems. In: 2011 IEEE Symposium on Large Data Analysis and Visualization (LDAV), October 2011

30. Whitlock, B., Favre, J.M., Meredith, J.S.: Parallel in situ coupling of simulation with a fully featured visualization system. In: Proceedings of the 11th Eurographics Conference on Parallel Graphics and Visualization, EGPGV 2011. Eurographics Association (2011)

31. Yu, H., Wang, C., Grout, R., Chen, J., Ma, K.L.: In situ visualization for large-scale combustion simulations. IEEE Comput. Graph. Appl. 3, 45–57 (2010)

32. Zhao, G., Perilla, J.R., Yufenyuy, E.L., Meng, X., Chen, B., Ning, J., Ahn, J., Gronenborn, A.M., Schulten, K., Aiken, C.: Mature HIV-1 capsid structure by cryo-electron microscopy and all-atom molecular dynamics. Nature 497, 643–646 (2013)

33. Zheng, F., Abbasi, H., Docan, C., Lofstead, J., Liu, Q., Klasky, S., Parashar, M., Podhorszki, N., Schwan, K., Wolf, M.: PreDatA - preparatory data analytics on peta-scale machines. In: 2010 IEEE International Symposium on Parallel Distributed Processing (IPDPS) (2010)

34. Zheng, F., Abbasi, H., Cao, J., Dayal, J., Schwan, K., Wolf, M., Klasky, S., Podhorszki, N.: In-situ I/O processing: a case for location flexibility. In: Proceedings of the Sixth Workshop on Parallel Data Storage, PDSW 2011, ACM, New York (2011)

35. Zheng, F., Yu, H., Hantas, C., Wolf, M., Eisenhauer, G., Schwan, K., Abbasi, H., Klasky, S.: Goldrush: resource efficient in situ scientific data analytics using fine-grained interference aware execution. In: Proceedings of the International Conference on High Performance Computing, Networking, Storage and Analysis, SC 2013. ACM (2013)
36. Zheng, F., Zou, H., Eisenhauer, G., Schwan, K., Wolf, M., Dayal, J., Nguyen, T.A., Cao, J., Abbasi, H., Klasky, S., Podhorszki, N., Yu, H.: FlexIO: I/O middleware for location-flexible scientific data analytics. In: Proceedings of the 2013 IEEE 27th International Symposium on Parallel and Distributed Processing, IPDPS 2013. IEEE Computer Society (2013)

Solving Linear Systems on the Intel Xeon-Phi Accelerator via the Gauss-Huard Algorithm

Ernesto Dufrechou[1]([⊠]), Pablo Ezzatti[1], Enrique S. Quintana-Ortí[2], and Alfredo Remón[3]

[1] Instituto de Computación, Universidad de la República, 11300 Montevideo, Uruguay
{edufrechou,pezzatti}@fing.edu.uy
[2] Departamento de Ingeniería y Ciencia de la Computación, Universidad Jaime I, 12701 Castellón, Spain
quintana@icc.uji.es
[3] Max Planck Institute for Dynamics of Complex Technical Systems, 30106 Magdeburg, Germany
remon@mpi-magdeburg.mpg.de

Abstract. The solution of linear systems is a key operation in many scientific and engineering applications. Traditional solvers are based on the LU factorization of the coefficient matrix, and optimized implementations of this method are available in well-known dense linear algebra libraries for most hardware architectures. The Gauss-Huard algorithm (GHA) is a reliable and alternative method that presents a computational effort close to that of the LU-based approach. In this work we present several implementations of GHA on the Intel Xeon Phi coprocessor. The experimental results show that our solvers based in GHA represent a competitive alternative to LU-based solvers, being an appealing method for the solution of small to medium linear systems, with remarkable reductions in the time-to-solution for systems of dimension $n \leq 4,000$.

Keywords: Dense linear systems · LU factorization · Gauss-Huard algorithm · Multi-core processors · Xeon Phi processor · High performance

1 Introduction

Many scientific and engineering applications require, as a key computational problem, the solution of a *linear system* of the form $Ax = b$, where $A \in \mathbb{R}^{n \times n}$ is the coefficient matrix, $b \in \mathbb{R}^n$ is the vector containing the independent terms, and vector $x \in \mathbb{R}^n$ stands for the sought-after solution [2]. When A is dense and large, the most popular approach to tackle this problem commences by decomposing this matrix into two triangular factors via the LU factorization (Gaussian elimination) [5]: $A = LU$, where $L, U \in \mathbb{R}^{n \times n}$ are respectively unit lower triangular and upper triangular. For numerical stability, partial row pivoting is

© Springer International Publishing Switzerland 2015
C. Osthoff et al. (Eds.): CARLA 2015, CCIS 565, pp. 107–117, 2015.
DOI: 10.1007/978-3-319-26928-3_8

in practice introduced during the initial factorization stage [5]. This is followed next by two triangular system solvers, involving the triangular factors L and U.

The Gauss-Jordan elimination (GJE), enhanced with partial row pivoting, is a numerically reliable alternative to Gaussian elimination for the solution of linear systems. However, this approach features a considerably higher computational cost, around n^3 floating-point arithmetic operations (flops) compared with the $2n^3/3$ flops of an LU-based solver. In 1979, P. Huard introduced a variant of GJE, hereafter referred to as the Gauss-Huard algorithm (GHA) [9], that solved this drawback, exhibiting a computational cost analogous to that of the LU-based method. Furthermore, GHA can be easily combined with partial column pivoting to yield a numerical stability that is comparable with that of the LU-based method with partial row pivoting [1].

Intel's "Knights Corner" Xeon Phi co-processor, built with 22 nm technology, has rapidly gained relevance among the high performance computing community. This many-core accelerator is present in five out of the 50 fastest supercomputers in the last Top500 list (dated July 2015) [10], including the system ranked in the top position, Tianhe-2, which offers 33.86 PFLOPS (quadrillions of flops per second) in the LINPACK benchmark. In addition to remarkable performance, Intel's current many-core coprocessor offers a wide range of well-known parallel programming interfaces as well as appealing energy efficiency (in terms of throughput-per-Watt), being a crucial component in several of the most energy-efficient supercomputers in the last Green500 list [6]. The future of this production line seems reinforced by the fact that Intel views the next generation of the Xeon Phi architecture, in 14 nm and codenamed as "Knights Landing", as a full server, enterprise-class, performant, reliable processor, which is far beyond the role of a simple co-processor.

A number of recent research efforts have demonstrated the benefits of leveraging the Intel Xeon Phi to accelerate the execution of complex dense linear algebra operations [3,4]. In this paper we further investigate the efficiency of the Intel Xeon Phi, presenting several implementations of the GHA with column pivoting to solve dense linear systems on this platform. Through careful optimization of our codes, the resulting GHA-based solver clearly outperforms the routine in Intel MKL library for the solution of dense linear systems of dimension $n \leq 5,000$.

The rest of the paper is structured as follows. In Sect. 2, we briefly review the LU-based and GHA approaches to solve linear systems. In Sect. 3, we present and evaluate several new solvers based on GHA for the Xeon Phi processor. Finally, we offer a few conclusions and discuss future work in Sect. 4.

2   Solution of Linear Systems

In this section we revisit the traditional LU-based approach and the GHA alternative for the solution of dense linear systems. Both methods proceed "in-place", overwriting the coefficient matrix with intermediate results and vector b with the solution x, and feature a similar cost in terms of flops and memory requirements.

2.1   The LU Factorization

This method commences by computing the LU factorization of matrix A. To ensure numerical stability, row pivoting is added during this decomposition [5] so that, in practice, the factorization adopts the form $PA = LU$, where $P \in \mathbb{R}^{n \times n}$ is a permutation matrix (implicitly stored as a vector), and the triangular factors $L, U \in \mathbb{R}^{n \times n}$ (unit lower triangular and upper triangular, respectively) overwrite the corresponding parts of A. Note that the diagonal of L consists of ones only and, therefore, it is unnecessary to store its entries explicitly. The original system is then equivalent to $LUx = (Pb) = \hat{b}$, and x can be obtained by solving the lower triangular linear system $Ly = \hat{b}$, for $y \in \mathbb{R}^n$, followed by the upper triangular system $Ux = y$.

The LU-based solver presents three properties that may negatively impact its performance. Concretely, the method is divided into three consecutive stages (LU factorization, lower triangular solve and upper triangular solve) which implicitly define two synchronization points. Furthermore, it requires the solution of two triangular linear systems, an operation that presents a rich collection of data dependencies and exhibits more reduced concurrency than other Level-3 BLAS kernels. Finally, a number of small triangular linear systems also appear during the factorization stage.

2.2   The Gauss-Huard Algorithm

The method underlying GHA is algorithmically captured in Fig. 1 using the FLAME notation [7]. In this algorithm, column pivoting simply requires that, right before the diagonalization of $\left[\hat{\alpha}_{11}, \; \hat{a}_{12}^T\right]$, (1) this vector is searched for its maximum entry in magnitude (excluding its last element, which contains an entry from b); and (2) the column of $\hat{A}$ corresponding to this entry is swapped with the column of $\hat{A}$ containing the diagonal entry $\hat{\alpha}_{11}$.

A blocked variant of GHA was introduced for distributed-memory (message-passing) systems in [8], but the authors did not perform any experimental evaluation of the implementation. They stated that its performance could be expected to be close to that of an LU-based solver, and also proposed a variant that merges the block-column elimination of one iteration with the block-row elimination of the following iteration into a single matrix multiplication.

The blocked version of GHA is given in Fig. 2. Given a user-defined algorithmic block size b, the algorithm processes b columns of the matrix per iteration of the loop body. The pivoting only requires the integration of an unblocked algorithm that includes this technique during the block diagonalization, and the application of the permutations resulting from this stage to the matrix columns before the subsequent block-column elimination.

Algorithm: $\boxed{\hat{A}, p} := \textsc{GaussHuard}\_\textsc{unb}(\hat{A})$

Partition $\hat{A} \to \left(\begin{array}{c|c} \hat{A}_{TL} & \hat{A}_{TR} \\ \hline \hat{A}_{BL} & \hat{A}_{BR} \end{array} \right), p \to \left(\begin{array}{c|c} p_L & p_R \end{array} \right)$

where $\hat{A}_{TL}, p_L$ are 0×0

while $m(\hat{A}_{TL}) < m(\hat{A})$ **do**

    Repartition

$$\left(\begin{array}{c|c} \hat{A}_{TL} & \hat{A}_{TR} \\ \hline \hat{A}_{BL} & \hat{A}_{BR} \end{array} \right) \to \left(\begin{array}{c|c|c} \hat{A}_{00} & \hat{a}_{01} & \hat{A}_{02} \\ \hline \hat{a}_{10}^T & \hat{\alpha}_{11} & \hat{a}_{12}^T \\ \hline \hat{A}_{20} & \hat{a}_{21} & \hat{A}_{22} \end{array} \right), \left(\begin{array}{c|c} p_L & p_R \end{array} \right) \to \left(\begin{array}{c|c|c} p_0 & \pi_1 & p_2 \end{array} \right)$$

    where $\hat{\alpha}_{11}, \pi_1$ are 1×1

$\left[\hat{\alpha}_{11}, \ \hat{a}_{12}^T \right] := \left[\hat{\alpha}_{11}, \ \hat{a}_{12}^T \right] - \hat{a}_{10}^T \cdot \left[\hat{a}_{01}, \ \hat{A}_{02} \right]$; Row elimination

$\pi_1 := \text{PivIndex}\left(\left[\hat{\alpha}_{11}, \ \hat{a}_{12}^T \right] \right)$

$\left(\begin{array}{c|c} \hat{a}_{01} & \hat{A}_{02} \\ \hline \hat{\alpha}_{11} & \hat{a}_{12}^T \\ \hline \hat{a}_{21} & \hat{A}_{22} \end{array} \right) := \left(\begin{array}{c|c} \hat{a}_{01} & \hat{A}_{02} \\ \hline \hat{\alpha}_{11} & \hat{a}_{12}^T \\ \hline \hat{a}_{21} & \hat{A}_{22} \end{array} \right) P(\pi_1)$; Pivoting

$\left[\hat{\alpha}_{11}, \ \hat{a}_{12}^T \right] := \left[\hat{\alpha}_{11}, \ \hat{a}_{12}^T \right] / \hat{\alpha}_{11}$; Diagonalization (row scaling)

$\hat{A}_{02} := \hat{A}_{02} - \hat{a}_{01} \cdot \hat{a}_{12}^T$; Column elimination

---

    Continue with

$$\left(\begin{array}{c|c} \hat{A}_{TL} & \hat{A}_{TR} \\ \hline \hat{A}_{BL} & \hat{A}_{BR} \end{array} \right) \leftarrow \left(\begin{array}{c|c|c} \hat{A}_{00} & \hat{a}_{01} & \hat{A}_{02} \\ \hline \hat{a}_{10}^T & \hat{\alpha}_{11} & \hat{a}_{12}^T \\ \hline \hat{A}_{20} & \hat{a}_{21} & \hat{A}_{22} \end{array} \right), \left(\begin{array}{c|c} p_L & p_R \end{array} \right) \leftarrow \left(\begin{array}{c|c|c} p_0 & \pi_1 & p_2 \end{array} \right)$$

endwhile

Fig. 1. Basic (unblocked) Gauss-Huard algorithm for the solution of $Ax = b$. On entry, $\hat{A} = [A, b]$. Upon completion, due to pivoting, the last column of $\hat{A}$ is overwritten with a permutation of the solution, $P(p)x$. In the notation, $m(\cdot)$ stands for the number of rows of its input. Furthermore, $\text{PivIndex}\left(\left[\hat{\alpha}_{11}, \ \hat{a}_{12}^T \right] \right)$ returns the index of the entry of largest magnitude in its input (excluding the last element, which corresponds to an entry of b); and $P(\pi_1)$ denotes the corresponding permutation.

3 Efficient Implementation of GHA on the Intel Xeon Phi Co-processor

3.1 Experimental Setup

All the implementations and experiments in this section employ IEEE double-precision arithmetic and were performed on a board equipped with an Intel Xeon Phi 7120 co-processor (61 cores and 16 GBytes of GDDR5 DRAM) attached to a server through a PCI-e Gen3 slot. The tests were ran in Intel's native execution mode and, therefore, the specifications of the server are irrelevant. The codes were compiled using the Intel icc v.15.0.1 compiler with the -O3 optimization flag. All the variants were linked with the Intel MKL v.11.2.1 library.

We tested the execution using 15, 30 and 60 of physical cores, with 1, 2 and 4 threads per core. We also experimented with three policies to map threads to cores: *compact*, *scatter* and *balanced*. In addition, we tested two values for the

Algorithm: $\left[\hat{A}, p\right] := \text{GaussHuard\_blk}(\hat{A})$

Partition $\hat{A} \rightarrow \left(\begin{array}{c|c} \hat{A}_{TL} & \hat{A}_{TR} \\ \hline \hat{A}_{BL} & \hat{A}_{BR} \end{array}\right), p \rightarrow \left(\begin{array}{c|c} p_L & p_R \end{array}\right)$

  where $\hat{A}_{TL}$ is 0×0 and p_L has 0 elements

while $m(\hat{A}_{TL}) < m(\hat{A})$ **do**
  Determine block size b
  Repartition

$$\left(\begin{array}{c|c} \hat{A}_{TL} & \hat{A}_{TR} \\ \hline \hat{A}_{BL} & \hat{A}_{BR} \end{array}\right) \rightarrow \left(\begin{array}{c|c|c} \hat{A}_{00} & \hat{A}_{01} & \hat{A}_{02} \\ \hline \hat{A}_{10} & \hat{A}_{11} & \hat{A}_{12} \\ \hline \hat{A}_{20} & \hat{A}_{21} & \hat{A}_{22} \end{array}\right), \left(\begin{array}{c|c} p_L & p_R \end{array}\right) \rightarrow \left(\begin{array}{c|c|c} p_0 & p_1 & p_2 \end{array}\right)$$

  where $\hat{A}_{11}$ is $b \times b$

$\left[\hat{A}_{11}, \ \hat{A}_{12}\right] := \left[\hat{A}_{11}, \ \hat{A}_{12}\right] - \hat{A}_{10} \cdot \left[\hat{A}_{01}, \ \hat{A}_{02}\right]$; Block-row elimination

$\left[\hat{A}_{11}, \ \hat{A}_{12}, p_1\right] := \text{GaussHuard\_unb}\left(\left[\hat{A}_{11}, \ \hat{A}_{12}\right]\right)$; Block diagonalization

$\left(\begin{array}{c|c} \hat{A}_{01} & \hat{A}_{02} \\ \hline & \\ \hline \hat{A}_{21} & \hat{A}_{22} \end{array}\right) := \left(\begin{array}{c|c} \hat{A}_{01} & \hat{A}_{02} \\ \hline & \\ \hline \hat{A}_{21} & \hat{A}_{22} \end{array}\right) P(p_1)$; Pivoting

$\hat{A}_{02} := \hat{A}_{02} - \hat{A}_{01} \cdot \hat{A}_{12}$; Block-column elimination

Continue with

$$\left(\begin{array}{c|c} \hat{A}_{TL} & \hat{A}_{TR} \\ \hline \hat{A}_{BL} & \hat{A}_{BR} \end{array}\right) \leftarrow \left(\begin{array}{c|c|c} \hat{A}_{00} & \hat{A}_{01} & \hat{A}_{02} \\ \hline \hat{A}_{10} & \hat{A}_{11} & \hat{A}_{12} \\ \hline \hat{A}_{20} & \hat{A}_{21} & \hat{A}_{22} \end{array}\right), \left(\begin{array}{c|c} p_L & p_R \end{array}\right) \leftarrow \left(\begin{array}{c|c|c} p_0 & p_1 & p_2 \end{array}\right)$$

endwhile

Fig. 2. Blocked Gauss-Huard algorithm for the solution of $Ax = b$. On entry, $\hat{A} = [A, b]$. Upon completion, due to pivoting, the last column of $\hat{A}$ is overwritten with a permutation of the solution, $P(p)x$.

algorithmic block size, $b = 32$ and 64. we only report the results corresponding to the combination of number of cores/threads, mapping policy (affinity) and algorithmic block size which offered the highest performance.

3.2 Baseline Implementation

As a starting point, we implemented the blocked GaussHuard_blk algorithm on the Intel Xeon Phi with the support from the native implementation of BLAS for this architecture in Intel MKL. In particular, the block-column and row eliminations can be performed via calls to kernel DGEMM for the matrix multiplication. The block diagonalization requires to implement the unblocked GaussHuard_unb algorithm, but most operations in this stage can also be cast in terms of the computational kernels in Intel MKL. In particular, kernels DGEMV, DSCAL and DGER provide the functionality necessary for the row elimination, diagonalization and the column elimination, respectively. Additionally, the pivoting strategy can be performed via kernels IDAMAX (to find the pivot) and DSWAP (to perform the column interchanges).

In this initial implementation, hereafter referred to as GaussHuard, a significant fraction of the flops are performed inside the highly parallel kernel DGEMM. In consequence, we can expect reasonable performance from this approach, with the exact level depending on the efficiency of the underlying implementation of DGEMM, among other factors.

Table 1. Execution times (in seconds) for the GaussHuard variant.

n	Block-row elim.	Block diag.	Block-column elim.	Others	Total
1,000	16	598	7	12	633
2,000	61	2,488	23	36	2,608
3,000	180	6,150	82	70	6,482
4,000	332	14,650	162	134	15,278
5,000	466	23,822	196	247	24,731

The results in Table 1 show that most of the computational time of this first variant is spent in the block diagonalization. Surprisingly, although a major part of the flops occur in the block-row and block-column elimination, both operations only represent about 3 % of the total computational time. In contrast, the block diagonalization takes about 95 % of the runtime, which is clearly much higher than its theoretical cost. A detailed study of this operation shows that the diagonalization–application of pivoting (performed via kernels DSCAL, IDAMAX and DSWAP) and the column elimination (via kernel DGER) consume about 30 % and 60 % of the time, respectively. Regarding the optimal setting, when $n \leq 4,000$ the best results are obtained with 30 cores, 2 threads per core (for a total of 60 threads), the *compact* affinity and $b = 32$. When $n = 5,000$, the best option is to employ the 60 cores, 2 threads/core, *compact* affinity and $b = 32$.

3.3   Improving via Matrix Transposition, GaussHuard_T

The experimentation with the GaussHuard implementation in the previous subsection exposes the urge to improve the block diagonalization, in particular, the operations comprised by the application of the pivoting strategy and column elimination. Although that implementation of the GAUSSHUARD_UNB algorithm relies on highly-tuned computational kernels from the Intel MKL library, a major source of overhead arises because of the row-wise accesses to matrix A whose entries, following the BLAS convention, are stored in column-major order. For example, with column pivoting, the IDAMAX kernel looks for the pivot within a row of the matrix, and the elements of this search space are separated in memory at least by n entries. This results in slow memory accesses in kernels that are, by definition, memory-bounded.

To tackle this drawback, we propose to apply the GHA to matrix $\hat{A}^T$. The new variant, named GaussHuard_T, requires to transpose matrix $\hat{A}$, to then apply

GHA on this transposed matrix. Thus, in the GaussHuard_T implementation, the updates in GaussHuard_unb algorithm are replaced by:

$$\begin{bmatrix} \hat{\alpha}_{11} \\ \hat{a}_{21} \end{bmatrix} := \begin{bmatrix} \hat{\alpha}_{11} \\ \hat{a}_{21} \end{bmatrix} - \begin{bmatrix} \hat{a}_{10}^T \\ \hat{A}_{20} \end{bmatrix} \cdot \hat{a}_{01},$$

$$\begin{bmatrix} \hat{\alpha}_{11} \\ \hat{a}_{21} \end{bmatrix} := \begin{bmatrix} \hat{\alpha}_{11} \\ \hat{a}_{21} \end{bmatrix} / \hat{\alpha}_{11}, \quad \text{and}$$

$$\hat{A}_{20} := \hat{A}_{20} - \hat{a}_{21} \cdot \hat{a}_{10}^T$$

Analogous changes are applied to the GaussHuard_blk algorithm, and in consequence, from the point of view of storage, GaussHuard_T integrates row pivoting instead of column pivoting.

Table 2. Execution times (in seconds) for the GaussHuard_T variant.

n	Block-row elim.	Block diag.	Block-column elim.	Others	Total
1,000	45	131	30	12	218
2,000	200	428	91	35	754
3,000	556	841	225	68	1,690
4,000	1,125	1,522	284	151	3,082
5,000	1,936	2,420	426	266	5,048

Table 2 reports higher performance for this second variant, with a reduction of execution time by a factor of up to 5× with respect to the first one. The computational results exhibit that, while the block diagonalization is clearly accelerated, the performance of the rest of the operations is degraded. The reason is that the computational kernels embedded in the block diagonalization benefit from the new memory access pattern, but unfortunately this type of access harms the performance of kernel DGEMM. In any case, with the new variant GaussHuard_T, the block diagonalization requires about 50 % of the execution time, which is still more than expected. A detailed evaluation of the block diagonalization shows that the time dedicated to diagonalization and pivoting is now about 5 % of the total time, which is satisfactory; but the column elimination represents 30 % of time, which is too much. In summary, the performance of GaussHuard_T is limited by the low arithmetic throughput attained by DGER during the column elimination, and additionally suffers from the performance degradation of the block-row and column elimination stages.

The best setup for this variant utilizes 30 cores, 60 threads (i.e., 2 per core), the *compact* affinity, and $b = 32$ when $n \le 3,000$. When $n \ge 4,000$, on the other hand, the best results are obtained with 120 threads.

3.4   Using OpenMP, GaussHuard_O

In this new variant we again aim to accelerate the block diagonalization. For this purpose, we discard the matrix transposition and replace the invocations to the

BLAS kernels which attain low performance (specifically IDAMAX, DSCAL, and DGER) by *ad-hoc* implementations that parallelize the corresponding operation via OpenMP directives.

Table 3. Execution times (in seconds) for the `GaussHuard_0` variant.

n	Block-row elim.	Block diag.	Block-column elim.	Others	Total
1,000	11	177	11	8	207
2,000	60	409	29	27	525
3,000	173	672	69	55	969
4,000	327	999	139	109	1,574
5,000	639	1,383	259	166	2,447

Table 3 shows the results obtained with the new `GaussHuard_0` solver. This variant outperforms the previous ones delivering important time reductions. The block diagonalization is drastically accelerated. Concretely, `GaussHuard_0` reports accelerating factors of up to 10× and 2× with respect to `GaussHuard` and `GaussHuard_T`, respectively. Unfortunately, a detailed evaluation shows that, despite of the effort, the block diagonalization still consumes half of the global time. In particular, the diagonalization and the pivoting-related operations take about 40 % of the execution time.

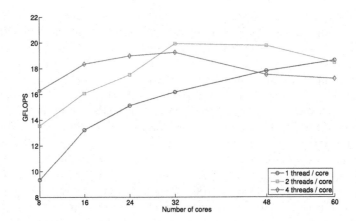

Fig. 3. Performance of `GaussHuard_0` with different configurations of the Xeon Phi.

The best results for this third variant are obtained with the *compact* affinity and $b = 32$. Figure 3 summarizes the performance of this variant for several configurations of the Xeon Phi processor, specifically, using different number of cores and different number of threads per core. The best performance is reported with 30 cores and 2 threads per core.

Table 4. Execution time (in milliseconds) of the GHA implementations and the Intel MKL solver on the Intel Xeon Phi.

n	GaussHuard	GaussHuard_T	GaussHuard_O	MKL
1,000	633	218	207	1,194
2,000	2,608	754	525	1,478
3,000	6,482	1,690	969	1,661
4,000	15,278	3,082	1,574	2,181
5,000	23,822	5,048	2,447	2,451

3.5   Global Evaluation

To conclude the experimental analysis, we compare the three GHA-based solvers against the routine in Intel MKL library for the solution of linear systems: DGESV. Table 4 reports the execution times obtained by the four solvers and Fig. 4 shows the corresponding accelerating factors (speed-ups) of the GHA-based solvers over the MKL counterpart. For this experiment, we executed DGESV with the same Xeon Phi configurations listed in the experimental setup. Namely, different number of cores and threads, and the three affinity policies, but we only report the results for the best option. The experiment reveals that the GHA variants outperform the LU-based solver in DGESV for small matrices. This can be explained because DGESV is a three-step method (factorization followed by two triangular solvers), and it thus integrates three synchronization points. Additionally, the triangular solves present two drawbacks: they work with a triangular matrix which hampers load balance and, furthermore, they correspond to memory-bound BLAS-2 operation. On the other hand, the performance of the GHA variants is constrained by that of the block-diagonalization operation when the problem dimension increases. Nevertheless, GaussHuard_O still outperforms the solver in MKL when the matrix dimension $n \leq 4,000$ and offers similar results when $n = 5,000$. For larger values, DGESV is the best option as the impact of the triangular solves in the global computational time becomes smaller as n grows, and in such scenario, the performance of the procedure then boils down to that of the factorization step.

Figure 5 shows the performance provided by the four solvers in terms of GFLOPS (billions of flops per second). We note that the performance of all solvers is far from the peak performance of the Intel Xeon Phi. However, this was expected as we target problems of small-to-moderate dimension. In most cases, the best performance is obtained using only half of the computational units and only 25 % of the supported threads in the platform. The performance attained by the GaussHuard variant is nearly the same for all the matrix sizes. This is because it is limited by the performance of the memory-bounded operations and, consequently, this variant presents a BLAS1-like behavior. The GaussHuard_T and GaussHuard_O versions partly solve this problem, especially GaussHuard_O. Finally, the Intel MKL implementation exhibits a BLAS3-like behavior and therefore, it is the most efficient variant for the solution of medium-to-large linear systems.

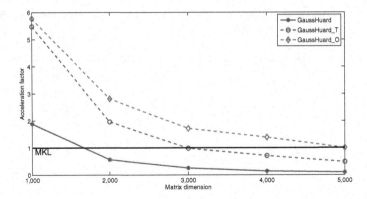

Fig. 4. Acceleration factors of the GHA implementations with respect to Intel MKL solver on the Intel Xeon Phi.

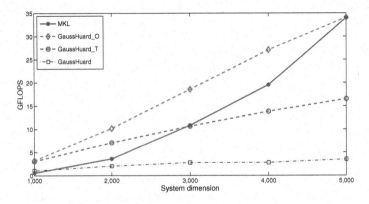

Fig. 5. Performance of the GHA implementations and the Intel MKL solver on the Intel Xeon Phi.

4   Concluding Remarks and Future Work

The Gauss-Huard algorithm (GHA), enhanced with partial column pivoting, is a reliable method to solve linear systems that presents arithmetic cost and numerical stability close to those of the LU-based method with partial row pivoting. In this work, we have introduced several implementations of GHA tailored for the Intel Xeon Phi co-processor. The experimental evaluation demonstrates that this method can offer competitive performance and, for small and moderate-size problems, even be faster than the optimized solver based on the LU factorization in Intel MKL.

As part of future work, we intend to further optimize the implementation using a more sophisticated double-blocking approach as well as incorporate further improvements to optimize the BLAS-1 and BLAS-2 operations that are necessary for pivoting. Moreover, we will extend our evaluation to assess the impact of the different Xeon Phi settings (number of cores, number of threads and affinity) in energy consumption.

Acknowledgments. The researcher from the *Universidad Jaime I* was supported by the CICYT projects TIN2011-23283 and TIN2014-53495-R of the *Ministerio de Economía y Competitividad* and FEDER. Ernesto Dufrechou, Pablo Ezzatti and Alfredo Remón were supported by the EHFARS project funded by the German Ministry of Education and Research BMBF.

References

1. Dekker, T.J., Hoffmann, W., Potma, K.: Stability of the Gauss-Huard algorithm with partial pivoting. Computing **58**, 225–244 (1997)
2. Demmel, J.W.: Applied Numerical Linear Algebra. Society for Industrial and Applied Mathematics, Philadelphia (1997)
3. Dolz, M.F., Igual, F.D., Ludwig, T., Piñuel, L., Quintana-Ortí, E.S.: Balancing task- and data-parallelism to improve performance and energy consumption of matrix computations on the Intel Xeon Phi. Comput. Electr. Eng. (2015, to appear)
4. Dongarra, J., Gates, M., Haidar, A., Jia, Y., Kabir, K., Luszczek, P., Tomov, S.: HPC programming on Intel many-integrated-core hardware with MAGMA port to Xeon Phi. Sci. Program. **2015**, 1–11 (2015). (ID 502593)
5. Golub, G.H., Van Loan, C.F.: Matrix Computations, 3rd edn. The Johns Hopkins University Press, Baltimore (1996)
6. GREEN500.org. http://www.green500.org/. Accessed July 2015
7. Gunnels, J.A., Gustavson, F.G., Henry, G.M., van de Geijn, R.A.: FLAME: formal linear algebra methods environment. ACM Trans. Math. Softw. **27**(4), 422–455 (2001)
8. Hoffmann, W., Potma, K., Pronk, G.: Solving dense linear systems by Gauss-Huard's method on a distributed memory system. Future Gener. Comput. Syst. **10**(2–3), 321–325 (1994)
9. Huard, P.: La méthode simplex sans inverse explicite. EDB Bull. Dir. Études Rech. Sér. C Math. Inform. **2**, 79–98 (1979)
10. TOP500.org. http://www.top500.org/. Accessed July 2015

On a Dynamic Scheduling Approach to Execute OpenCL Jobs on APUs

Tiago Marques do Nascimento, Rodrigo Weber dos Santos,
and Marcelo Lobosco[✉]

FISIOCOMP, Laboratory of Computational Physiology and High-Performance
Computing, DCC, ICE, UFJF, Campus Universitário,
Juiz de Fora, MG 36036-900, Brazil
tiago.nascimento@uab.ufjf.br, {rodrigo.weber,marcelo.lobosco}@ufjf.edu.br
http://www.fisiocomp.ufjf.br

Abstract. This work presents a dynamic scheduling approach used to
load balance the computation between CPU and GPU of an Accelerated
Processing Unit (APU). The results have shown that the dynamic load
balancing strategy was successful in reducing the computation time of an
Human Immune System (HIS) simulator that was used as benchmark.
The dynamic scheduling approach accelerate the HIS code up to 7 times
when compared to the parallel version that executes using only the CPU
cores, up to 32 % when compared to the parallel version that uses only
the GPU cores, and up to 9 % when compared to our previous static
scheduling approach.

Keywords: Load balancing · OpenCL · APUs

1 Introduction

An Accelerated Processing Unit (APU) [2] is a processor that embeds a CPU
(central processing unit) and a GPU (graphics processing unit) on a unique
silicon chip. From an architectural perspective, CPUs and GPUs were built
based on completely different philosophies [6]. The general-purpose CPU has
been designed to run many distinct types of applications and is composed by
multiple cores that can be used to process multiple tasks simultaneously or
even process multiple data in parallel. Superscalar pipelines, large multi-level
caches, branch prediction, and out-of-order execution were the main design techniques responsible for improving the performance of CPUs. The cost of such
improvements is the complexity of the processor control path as well as the die
area required to implement them, which in turn reduces the number of cores
that can be packed in a single chip. GPUs were initially built specifically for
rendering and other graphics applications. They are composed by hundreds or
even thousands of small and simple processing elements. The massive processing capability of GPUs draw the attention of programmers that started to use
GPUs also to execute general purpose computing, which gave rise to the GPGPU

© Springer International Publishing Switzerland 2015
C. Osthoff et al. (Eds.): CARLA 2015, CCIS 565, pp. 118–128, 2015.
DOI: 10.1007/978-3-319-26928-3_9

(General-Purpose computation on GPUs) field [12]. In particular, applications with a large degree of data parallelism can benefit from executing in such platform.

Although a large number of computing devices are available for use on the APU, since it integrates CPUs and GPUs, it can be hard to use all of then simultaneously to execute a single task in parallel due to their heterogeneous nature. In fact, heterogeneous computing on CPUs and GPUs using architectures like CUDA [8] and OpenCL [15] has fixed the roles for each device: GPUs have been used to handle data parallel work while CPUs handle all the rest. The CPU does not block after starting a computation on the GPU, so it could also handle part of the data parallel work submitted to the GPU, however it is not common to observe this alternative, specially if data dependency exists in the code executed on GPUs and CPUs. The use of this fixed role model under utilizes the system, since CPUs are idle while GPUs are computing.

In a previous work [16], OpenCL has been used to implement the parallel version of a mathematical model [18] that describes part of the Human Immune System (HIS). The code executed simultaneously on all CPU and GPU cores available for use in an APU: 4 CPUs cores and 384 GPUs cores. In order to deal with the heterogeneity of the APU architecture, a load balancing strategy was proposed. It was reported that the use of all devices available accelerate the code up to 6 times when compared to the parallel version that executes using only the four CPU cores and about 28 % when compared to the parallel version that uses only the 384 GPU cores. Also, the load balancing strategy proposed was able to accelerate the code about 3.7 times when compared to the unbalanced version of the code that uses all CPU and CPU cores available.

This work further extends the previous load balancing strategy used. In the previous version [16] load balancing was achieved as follows. For the first one percent of the time steps, both GPU and CPU received a given amount of data and the time required to compute them, including the time spent in communication, was recorded. Based on their execution time, the values used for data partition were computed. These values were then used for the remaining time steps. In this work we adopted a dynamic approach that allows data partition to change during execution. The new approach improves performance up to 9 %, when compared to the previous static partition approach.

The remaining of this work is organized as follows. Section 2 presents the related work. Section 3 presents OpenCL in short. Section 4 presents the implementation details of the new approach and Sect. 5 presents the results obtained using the HIS simulator as a benchmark. Finally, the last Section presents the conclusions and plans for future works.

2   Related Work

Harmony [3] is a runtime supported programming and execution model that uses a data dependency graph to schedule and run independent kernels in parallel heterogeneous architectures. This approach is distinct from ours because we focus on data parallelism, while Harmony focus on task parallelism. Merge [11] is a library system that deals with map-reduce applications on heterogeneous system. Qilin [13] is an API that automatically partitions threads to one CPU and one GPU. SKMD [9] is a framework that transparently distributes the work of a single parallel kernel across CPUs and GPUs. SOCL [7] is an OpenCL implementation that allows users to dynamically dispatch kernels over devices. StarPu [1] is a task programming library for hybrid architectures that provides support for heterogeneous scheduling, but unfortunately it does not support APUs. Our approach is distinct because we are not proposing a new library, API, framework or OpenCL implementation, nor we limit the number of CPUs or GPUs that can be used as Qilin does. Since the proposed dynamic scheduling approach is implemented in the application code, we do not have to pay the overheads imposed by the frameworks, runtime systems or APIs.

3   OpenCL

OpenCL (Open Computing Language) [15] is a standard framework created by the industry (Khronos Group) in order to help the development of parallel applications that execute in heterogeneous systems, composed by a combination of CPUs, GPUs, and other processors/accelerators. The first release of OpenCL was in December of 2008, and its last release is OpenCL 2.0.

OpenCL devices such as CPUs, GPUs, and so on, execute the program instructions, called kernels. An OpenCL device is composed by compute units, which can further be divided into processing elements(PEs). The computation is carried on by these PEs. The following steps generalize the actions an application must follow in order to execute on an heterogeneous platform [15]:

1. Find all components that composes an heterogeneous platform;
2. Probe the characteristics of each component of the platform;
3. Create a context, that is, an environment where kernels will be executed;
4. Create the kernels that will execute on such contexts and devices;
5. Create and configure the command-queues, memory and parameters;
6. Invoke the kernels;
7. Collect the results.

An OpenCL platform includes a host, which is responsible for interacting with the user program. The interaction between the host and the devices is done using a command-queue. Commands are sent to the command-queue and wait there until they are executed on a device. There are three types of commands that can be issued: kernel execution, memory and synchronization commands. The commands within a single queue can execute in the same order they appear in the command-queue (in-order execution), or out-of-order. The programmer can enforce an order constrain using explicit synchronization mechanisms. Command-queues, specially those that implements the out-of-order execution, can be used to implement an automatic load balancing scheme based on the master-worker parallel pattern [14,15]. However, the master-worker parallel pattern is particularly suited for problems based on task parallelism [14]. In a previous work [16] we proposed a distinct solution based on an in-order execution for problems based on data parallelism and in this work we further improved the proposed solution.

4   Dynamic Scheduling

One key aspect of the parallel implementation on heterogeneous devices is data partition between devices. Since the number of GPU cores is much larger than the number of CPU cores, as well as GPU cores were tailored to execute programs that follows the SIMD model, load balancing must be used to ensure that no device is idle while other are overload. Data is split into two parts, one of which will be computed by the CPU, while the other one will be computed by the GPU, both using the same kernel code. The amount of data that will be assigned to the CPU and GPU depends on their relative computing capabilities.

Dynamic load balancing is achieved as follows. For each one percent of the time steps, both GPU and CPU receive a given amount of data and the time required to compute them, including the time spent in communication, is recorded. For the first time step, the initial amount of data that the GPU and the CPU will receive can be configured by the user; for the remaining time steps the division computed in the previous time step is used. Based on their execution time, the value of data division that will be used in the next time step, or even in the remaining computation steps, is computed using the Eq. 1:

$$P_G = \frac{T_c}{(T_g + T_c)} \tag{1}$$

where T_c is given by:

$$T_c = T_{CPU} \times P_{CPU} \tag{2}$$

and T_g is given by:

$$T_g = T_{GPU} \times P_{GPU} \tag{3}$$

P_G is the percentage of data that the GPU will receive to compute the next one percent of the time steps, so $1 - P_G$ is the percentage that the CPU will receive. T_{CPU} and T_{GPU} are respectively the time CPU and GPU spent to compute their data for the previous one percent of the time steps and P_{CPU} and P_{GPU} are respectively the percentage of data that CPU and GPU received to compute in the previous time step.

This process is repeated for each one percent of the time steps or until P_G does not change its value by more than a given threshold. In this work this value is equal to 1 %.

In our previous approach [16], only the first one percent of the time steps were used to find the values for data partition. For this reason, we will refer to it as static approach. At first, it is expected that the static approach should perform better on regular computations, while dynamic approach should perform better on irregular ones.

5   Numerical Results

5.1   Benchmark

To evaluate the performance of the dynamic scheduling approach, a simulator of the Human Immune System was used [17,18]. A set of eight Partial Differential Equations (PDEs) are used to describe this model, and simulate the temporal and spatial behavior of lipopolysaccharide (LPS), that represents an antigen in our model, as well as some cells and molecules involved in the innate immune response, such as neutrophils, macrophages, pro- and anti-inflammatory cytokines, and protein granules. The diffusion of some cells and molecules are described by the mathematical model, as well as the process of chemotaxis. Chemotaxis is the movement of immune cells in response to chemical stimuli by pro-inflammatory cytokine. Neutrophils and macrophages move towards the gradient of pro-inflammatory cytokine concentration. A detailed discussion about the model can be found in [17,18].

The numerical method used in the computational implementation of the mathematical model was the Finite Difference Method [10], a method commonly used in the numeric discretization of PDEs. The computation of the convective term (the chemotaxis term) is a complex part in the resolution of the PDEs. The development of numerical methods to approximate convective terms (in most cases non linear) have been subject of intense researches [5]. Our implementation is based on the finite difference method for the spatial discretization and the explicit Euler method for the time evolution. First-Order Upwind scheme [4] is used in the discretization of the chemotaxis term. Therefore, the precision of our numerical implementation is first-order in time (explicit Euler) and first-order in space (upwind scheme). The upwind scheme discretizes the hyperbolic PDEs through the use of differences with bias in the direction given by the signal of the characteristics' speeds. The upwind scheme uses an adaptive or solution-sensitive stencil to numerically simulate more precisely the direction of information propagation. More details about the numerical implementation, specially how the Laplace operator, that simulates the diffusion phenomenon, is implemented in 3D, can be found in one of our previous work [18]. This previous work used C and CUDA in the implementation, while this work uses C and OpenCL.

The numerical methods used in this work are regular but requires that, at each time step, processes that execute on CPU have access to the points computed by the GPU on the previous time step, and vice-versa. These points are called border points. The exchange of border points between CPU and GPU requires the introduction of synchronization operations and the explicit copy of data. Synchronization is done using OpenCL *clFinish* function. This function blocks execution until all previously queued OpenCL commands have completed. Both data copy and synchronization operations are expensive and deteriorate performance and should be avoided.

5.2 Computational Platform

Computational experiments were performed on an A10-5800K Radeon APU. A10-5800K is composed by one CPU and one GPU. The CPU has four 3.8 GHz cores, with 16 KB of L1 data cache per core, and 2×2 MB of L2 cache, so two cores share a single L2 cache. The GPU has 384 cores running at 800 MHz. The system has 16 GB of main memory, 2 GB of which are assigned to the exclusive use of the GPU. Unfortunately this APU model does not allow true memory sharing between CPU and GPU, in the sense that memory operations such as loads and stores cannot be used to establish direct communication between processes running on the CPU and GPU. Instead, explicit memory copy operations implemented in OpenCL API must be used to exchange data between processes on CPU and GPU. The machine runs Linux 3.11.0-15. OpenCL version 1.2 AMD and gcc version 4.6.3 were used to compile the codes.

5.3 Results

In order to evaluate the performance of the HIS application on the APU, four mesh sizes were used: $50 \times 50 \times 50$, $100 \times 100 \times 100$, $150 \times 150 \times 150$ and $200 \times 200 \times 200$. The memory required to execute the simulations using these mesh sizes range from about 7.7 MB to 488.3 MB, which is much lower than the total amount of memory available in the GPU.

The values used for initial conditions and to set all parameters used in the simulations are the same used in our previous work [16].

Five parallel versions of the code were developed: the first one uses only the CPU cores (CPU), the second version uses only the GPU (GPU), the third version uses both CPU and GPU, but it does not use any load balancing scheme (CPU+GPU), the fourth version uses the static scheme to balance the load between CPU and GPU cores (CPU+GPU+LBS) [16] while the last one uses the dynamic scheme proposed in this work (CPU+GPU+LBD). Border transfers occur only in the CPU+GPU, CPU+GPU+LBS and CPU+GPU+LBD versions. Since the execution time of each time step of the simulation is extremely regular, for all parallel versions we used $10,000$ simulation time steps to measure their execution time. The original simulator demands more than $1,000,000$ of time steps. For the CPU+GPU+LBS and CPU+GPU+LBD, the initial values used for P_{CPU} and P_{GPU} were 30 % and 70 %, respectively. This value changes along the execution of the code according to the load-balancing scheme used. In the CPU+GPU version, data is divided equally between CPU and GPU. All values obtained were compared against the results of the sequential version of the code, and all of them were correct.

Table 1 presents the execution time and the gains compared with the parallel version executed in the CPU. All versions were executed at least 5 times, and the standard deviations were all below 1.8 %.

At first, we would expect that the versions that use more computational resources (CPU+GPU, CPU+GPU+LBS and CPU+GPU+LBD) would achieve a better performance. In fact, as can be observed in Table 1, for all mesh size, the

Table 1. Experimental results for the parallel version of the code. Table presents, respectively, execution time(s) and the gains relative to the parallel CPU version of the code.

Version	$50 \times 50 \times 50$	$100 \times 100 \times 100$	$150 \times 150 \times 150$	$200 \times 200 \times 200$
CPU	324/-	2,542/-	6,516/-	13,320/-
GPU	59/5.5	422/6.0	1,380/4.7	3,576/3.7
CPU+GPU	79/4.1	841/3.0	3,809/1.7	9,211/1.4
CPU+GPU+LBS	49/6.6	369/6.9	1,222/5.3	2,930/4.5
CPU+GPU+LBD	46/7.1	356/7.1	1,121/5.8	2,715/4.9

best results were obtained by the CPU+GPU+LBD version of the code: 7.1, 7.1, 5.8 and 4.9 times faster than the parallel version of the code that executes on the CPU. As one can observe, the speedup decreases as the mesh size increases. The same can be observed in the versions of the code that executes only on the GPU and in the CPU+GPU+LBS version. These results indicate that the GPU already reached its saturation point. Recall that this GPU has only 384 cores available for use.

Compared to the version that uses only the GPU, CPU+GPU+LBD improved the performance by a factor from 19% to 32%. This result would not be possible without the use of the load balancing strategy proposed in this work, since the version that does not use load balancing performs worse than the GPU version of the code.

Finally, the dynamic approach outperforms the static one by a factor from 3.8% to 9%. The result is good, and better than we expected to achieve because: (a) the computation is the same in every iteration and (b) the dynamic approach imposes an overhead at each 1% of the time step till the amount of data that will be assigned to the CPU and GPU do not change more than a threshold from the previous step. For this benchmark, we observed that this occurs near 8% of the total time steps, and we were expecting that using 1% of the time steps, as the static approach does, should be enough to capture the best load to be assigned to each device.

In order to investigate why the static approach performed worst, we executed the OpenCL profile tool to collect extra information about the execution. Table 2 presents the figures obtained.

As one could expect from the results presented in Table 1, the dynamic approach improved the balance between CPU and GPU: CPU was idle waiting for the GPU finish its computation only 4.7% of the time, against 7.8% in the static approach. It must be stressed that to achieve an idle time equal to 0% is quite difficult because the amount of data that will be assigned to CPUs and GPUs consider the number of planes in $X \times Y \times Z$, not the total number of elements to be computed. Since a plane is composed by thousands of elements, a unique plane can be responsible for the imbalance between CPUs and GPUs. So to achieve a value closer to 0% the granularity used in data division should

Table 2. Profile data collected for the execution of the HIS simulator using a mesh size equal to $50 \times 50 \times 50$. Total memory time is the sum of read and write times. Times in *ms*.

Profile data	CPU+GPU+LBS	CPU+GPU+LBD
CPU/GPU rate (%)	92.2	95.3
Total read time	777	672
Amount of data read	20.7 MB	23.1 MB
Total write time	244	302
Amount of data written	28.4 MB	38 MB
Total memory time	1,021	975
clBuildProgram	549	553
L1 Data cache misses	4.1 %	3.4 %
L1 Instruction cache misses	5.4 %	6 %
L2 cache misses	3.7 %	3.9 %

be the individual elements to be computed, not the planes. However problems to aggregate communication on the GPU could occur due to memory misalignment. This point should be better investigate in future, since memory misalignment would occur only for part of the threads computing data in the plane shared by CPUs and GPUs.

Neither memory access times nor cache misses does help to explain why the dynamic load balancing approach performed better since the values are closer to the ones obtained by the static strategy. In fact the total amount of data transfers in the dynamic approach is higher, as could be expected, but it does not translates in higher total memory time. It should also be noted that the OpenCL function *clBuildProgram* is responsible by about 1 % of the total execution time. About 98 % of the time is spent executing the kernel. The invocation of the OpenCL function *clBuildProgram* causes the program object to be built for the list of devices that is called with, and is equivalent to invoking a compiler in a programming language [15].

Another possible cause to the worst performance of the static load balancing approach is the precision of the *time* function used to measure the time spent to execute 1 % of the iterations. For 10,000 time steps, 1 % of the time steps is equal to 100. Each time step demands about $4.2 - 4.6$ ms, so small variations on the execution of the 100 time steps could lead to a non optimum data division between devices. Although the dynamic approach uses the same percentage value for the time steps to decide which amount of data will be computed by the CPUs and GPUs, it can change this value through the computation to improve the performance. A final test was performed in order to investigate this hypothesis. It consists of the following steps. First, we investigate if the dynamic approach finds a static data division and, if so, how many steps were necessary to find it. As stated above, after 8 % of the time steps the value found for data division remains the same. In the second step we use a value above the one found in the previous step, for example, 10 %, in the static approach. More specifically, for the first ten percent of the time steps, both GPU and CPU receive a given amount of data and the time required to compute them is recorded. Based on their execution time, the optimal values of data division that will be used in the remaining 90 % of the computation steps is computed. Using 10 % of the iterations to define the data division reduces the total computation time from 49 s to 47 s, a value closer to that obtained by the dynamic approach, 46 s. The division found was 69.8 % of the planes to be computed by the GPUs and 30.2 % by the CPUs. As a reference, when using 1 % of the time steps to find the division, the values found where 77 % to the GPU and the remaining to the CPU. The dynamic approach found 68.2 % to the GPU. The 1 s of difference between the static and dynamic versions can also be explained for the cost to compute the first 10 % of the time steps. While the static approach uses a non-optimal initial value to compute them, the dynamic approach uses this initial value only for the first 1 % of the time steps, and then uses improved divisions for each one of the remaining time steps.

6   Conclusion and Future Works

In order to deal with the heterogeneity of the APU architecture, this work proposed and implemented a dynamic load balancing strategy. A parallel implementation of a mathematical model that describes part of the Human Immune System (HIS) was used to evaluate the proposed load balancing strategy.

The results have shown that the dynamic load balancing strategy was successful in reducing the computation time of the HIS simulations in all mesh sizes used: $50 \times 50 \times 50$, $100 \times 100 \times 100$, $150 \times 150 \times 150$ and $200 \times 200 \times 200$. The CPU+GPU+LBD version accelerate the code up to 7 times when compared to the parallel version that executes using only the CPU cores and up to 32 % when compared to the parallel version that uses only the GPU cores. Also, the load balancing strategy implemented was able to accelerate the code up to 9 % when compared to the version of the code that uses a static approach.

As future works, we plan to evaluate the proposed load balancing strategy using other benchmarks as well as in other architectures. In special, we plan to evaluate our strategy in two machines/scenarios. The first one is a machine that allows the use of shared memory to communicate processes that execute in CPU and GPU, which could eliminate the border transfer overhead, improving performance even more. In addition, we plan to evaluate our strategy in a machine with additional dedicated GPU devices. Although the machine used in the experiments has an additional dedicated GPU (Radeon 7700 series), it could not be used in the experiments because the APU's FM2 motherboard architecture does not allow the simultaneous use of the integrated GPU presented in the APU with the dedicated GPU, a feature only available, for example, in the FM2+ motherboard model.

Finally, we plan to investigate the use of individual elements, instead of planes, in data division and the use of a variable percentage to define the number of steps to be used to compute the data division. The idea is to increase the number of time steps automatically if the computing time for those time steps is lower than a given threshold.

Acknowledgments. The authors would like to thank UFJF and the Brazilian agencies CAPES, CNPq, FAPEMIG, and FINEP.

References

1. Augonnet, C., Thibault, S., Namyst, R., Wacrenier, P.A.: Starpu: a unified platform for task scheduling on heterogeneous multicore architectures. Concurr. Comput. Pract. Exper. **23**(2), 187–198 (2011). http://dx.doi.org/10.1002/cpe.1631
2. Branover, A., Foley, D., Steinman, M.: Amd fusion apu: Llano. IEEE Micro **32**(2), 28–37 (2012)
3. Diamos, G.F., Yalamanchili, S.: Harmony: an execution model and runtime for heterogeneous many core systems. In: Proceedings of the 17th International Symposium on High Performance Distributed Computing, HPDC 2008, pp. 197–200. ACM, New York (2008). http://doi.acm.org/10.1145/1383422.1383447
4. Hafez, M.M., Chattot, J.J.: Innovative Methods for Numerical Solution of Partial Differential Equations. World Scientific Publishing Company, New Jersey (2002)
5. Harten, A.: High resolution schemes for hyperbolic conservation laws. J. Comput. Phys. **135**, 260–278 (1997)
6. Hennessy, J.L., Patterson, D.A.: Computer Architecture: A Quantitative Approach, 5th edn. Morgan Kaufmann Publishers Inc., San Francisco (2011)
7. Henry, S., Denis, A., Barthou, D., Counilh, M.-C., Namyst, R.: Toward OpenCL automatic multi-device support. In: Silva, F., Dutra, I., Santos Costa, V. (eds.) Euro-Par 2014. LNCS, vol. 8632, pp. 776–787. Springer, Heidelberg (2014)
8. Kirk, D.B., Hwu, W.M.W.: Programming Massively Parallel Processors: A Hands-on Approach, 2nd edn. Morgan Kaufmann Publishers Inc., San Francisco (2013)
9. Lee, J., Samadi, M., Park, Y., Mahlke, S.: Transparent CPU-GPU collaboration for data-parallel kernels on heterogeneous systems. In: Proceedings of the 22nd International Conference on Parallel Architectures and Compilation Techniques, PACT 2013, pp. 245–256. IEEE Press, Piscataway (2013). http://dl.acm.org/citation.cfm?id=2523721.2523756
10. LeVeque, R.: Finite Difference Methods for Ordinary and Partial Differential Equations: Steady-State and Time-Dependent Problems (Classics in Applied Mathematics Classics in Applied Mathemat). Society for Industrial and Applied Mathematics, Philadelphia (2007)
11. Linderman, M.D., Collins, J.D., Wang, H., Meng, T.H.: Merge: a programming model for heterogeneous multi-core systems. In: Proceedings of the 13th International Conference on Architectural Support for Programming Languages and Operating Systems, ASPLOS XIII, pp. 287–296. ACM, New York (2008). http://doi.acm.org/10.1145/1346281.1346318
12. Luebke, D., Harris, M., Govindaraju, N., Lefohn, A., Houston, M., Owens, J., Segal, M., Papakipos, M., Buck, I.: Gpgpu: general-purpose computation on graphics hardware. In: Proceedings of the 2006 ACM/IEEE Conference on Supercomputing, SC 2006. ACM, New York (2006). http://doi.acm.org/10.1145/1188455.1188672

13. Luk, C.K., Hong, S., Kim, H.: Qilin: exploiting parallelism on heterogeneous multi-processors with adaptive mapping. In: Proceedings of the 42nd Annual IEEE/ACM International Symposium on Microarchitecture, MICRO 42, pp. 45–55. ACM, New York (2009). http://doi.acm.org/10.1145/1669112.1669121
14. Mattson, T., Sanders, B., Massingill, B.: Patterns for Parallel Programming, 1st edn. Addison-Wesley Professional, Boston (2004)
15. Munshi, A., Gaster, B., Mattson, T.G., Fung, J., Ginsburg, D.: OpenCL Programming Guide, 1st edn. Addison-Wesley Professional, Boston (2011)
16. do Nascimento, T.M., de Oliveira, J.M., Xavier, M.P., Pigozzo, A.B., dos Santos, R.W., Lobosco, M.: On the use of multiple heterogeneous devices to speedup the execution of a computational model of the human immune system. Appl. Math. Comput. **267**, 304–313 (2015)
17. Pigozzo, A.B., Macedo, G.C., Santos, R.W., Lobosco, M.: On the computational modeling of the innate immune system. BMC Bioinform. **14**(suppl. 6), S7 (2013)
18. Rocha, P.A.F., Xavier, M.P., Pigozzo, A.B., de M. Quintela, B., Macedo, G.C., dos Santos, R.W., Lobosco, M.: A three-dimensional computational model of the innate immune system. In: Murgante, B., Gervasi, O., Misra, S., Nedjah, N., Rocha, A.M.A.C., Taniar, D., Apduhan, B.O. (eds.) ICCSA 2012, Part I. LNCS, vol. 7333, pp. 691–706. Springer, Heidelberg (2012)

Scientific Computing Applications

Fine-Tuning Xeon Architecture Vectorization and Parallelization of a Numerical Method for Convection-Diffusion Equations

Frederico Luís Cabral[1]([⊠]), Carla Osthoff[1],
Diego Brandão[2], and Mauricio Kischinhevsky[3]

[1] Laboratório Nacional de Computação Científica, Petrópolis, RJ, Brazil
`fcabral@lncc.br`
[2] CEFET-RJ, São Gonçalo, RJ, Brazil
`diegonb.uff@gmail.com`
[3] Universidade Federal Fluminense, Niterói, RJ, Brazil
`kisch@ic.uff.br`

Abstract. This work describes the optimization process to improve the performance from a convection-diffusion equation from the HOPMOC method, on the Xeon architecture through the help Intel (r) tools, Vtune Amplifier, Compiler Reports and Intel Advisor. HOPMOC is a finite diffrence method to solve parabolic equations with convective dominance on a cluster with multiple multicore nodes. The method is based both on the modified method of characteristics and the Hopscotch method, it is implemented through an explicit-implicit operator splitting technique. This work studies the vectorization and parallelization version from HOPMOC under a Xeon processor architecture, and shows performance improvements up to 2 times per core, due to optimization via vectorization techniques and a gain up to 30 times on a 54 core environment, due to parallel strategies, compared to the sequential code.

Keywords: Parallel computing · HOPMOC method · Convection-diffusion equation · Intel XEON Processor · Vectorization · VTune Amplifier

1 Introduction

The need for fast solution of large scientific and industrial problems has long motivated the quest for improvements both in software as well as in hardware, since the inception of computing tools. In this context, vectorization, parallelization of tasks have been important strategies for the improvement of hardware efficiency during the last decades. Operator splitting techniques for the numerical solution of partial differential equations are also an attempt towards the same goal, on the software side. Effective and efficient architecture-driven techniques are sought for the efficient computation of accurate approximate solutions of systems of partial differential equations which describe a wide variety of phenomena.

© Springer International Publishing Switzerland 2015
C. Osthoff et al. (Eds.): CARLA 2015, CCIS 565, pp. 131–144, 2015.
DOI: 10.1007/978-3-319-26928-3_10

HOPMOC method was proposed as a method to solve parabolic problems with convective dominance in parallel machines [1]. This algorithm addresses the issue of parallelization from the beginning, by devising a spatial decoupling that allows the minimization of message-passing. It is direct in the sense that the cost per time step is known a priori, and uses a strategy based on tracking along the characteristics during the time-stepping. Operator splitting techniques, as the HOPMOC method, have been studied for the last decades, always as a means of reducing computational costs for multidimensional time dependent partial differential equations [2–4].

A sequential version of the HOPMOC method was employed to solve a convection diffusion equation in [9]. Furthermore, the necessary conditions to guarantee the HOPMOC stability are presented in [10]. A first MPI version of this method was implemented in [11], but it did not use a multicore cluster. HOPMOC has been studied on distributed memory machines under MPI, on multicore clusters under hybrid MPI/OpenMP and clusters with GPUs under Hybrid programming models [17].

The drive for vectorization in CPU chips started with the development of Intel MMX architectures. The MMX chip contained registers capable of parallel integer computations across eight (8) elements using a Single Instruction Multiple Data streams (SIMD) parallelization paradigm. The development of the MMX core was driven by the need to support graphics and other media acceleration, which is well suited for application to parallel computing using SIMD style approaches. While such integer operations were deemed sufficient at the time, the need for increased precision in these vector computations drove AMD to develop 3DNOW, after which Intel developed SSE the Streaming SIMD Extensions, both of which were capable of vectorized parallel computing across four floating point registers. For many years, researchers and computer scientists employed SSE to increase the performance of their codes through the parallelization of loops within their codes with the subsequent versions of SSE, each of which had increased usability and function support.

In 2008, Intel began the development of the next generation of in-core SIMD acceleration, naming their creation the Advanced Vector eXtensions (AVX). The concept was to double the size of registers available for vector computing, essentially increase the support for parallel computation from four (4) to eight (8) floating point variables. The first version of AVX was supported by the recently released Sandy Bridge (Intel) and Bulldozer (AMD) CPU cores, both released in 2011. In theory, this greatly increases the capacity for modern single CPU cores to perform limited parallel computation more or less strictly under the SIMD parallelization paradigm [1]. This development, together with the fact that many modern CPU chips contain multiple cores on each die, mean that a hybrid system of parallelization is required to take advantage of the computational power provided by modern cores. Intel AVX2 was released in 2013 with the fourth generation Intel Core processor family and further extends the breadth of vector processing capability across floating-point and integer data domains. This results in higher performance and more efficient data management across a wide range of applications like image and audio/video processing, scientific simulations, financial analytics and 3D modeling and analysis.

This paper describes the optimization process to improve the performance from a convection-diffusion equation from the HOPMOC method, on the Xeon architecture through the help of Vtune Amplifier, Compiler Reports and Intel Advisor for multithreading. It studies the vectorization and parallelization version from HOPMOC under a Xeon processor architecture, and shows performance improvements up to 2 times per core, compared to the sequential code. Also, parallelism brings an extra gain of performance by taking advantaged of multicore and manycore architectures.

The paper is organized as follows. Section 2 discusses the HOPMOC Method and its convergence features. Section 3 describes the parallel platform used in this study and shows a quick a description of our problem. Section 4 discusses optimization techniques such as vectorization and parallelization for the HOPMOC method, using hints given by VTune analysis. Section 5 presents some conclusions and indicates some new venues.

2   HOPMOC Method

Consider the one dimensional convection-diffusion equation in the form

$$u_t + v u_x = d u_{xx}, \tag{1}$$

with adequate initial and boundary conditions, where v is the constant and positive velocity, d is the constant and positive diffusivity, $0 \leq x \leq 1$ and $0 \leq t \leq T$. Consider a conventional finite difference discretization for this problem, where $\Delta t = t_{n+2} - t_n$, $\delta t = \frac{\Delta t}{2} = t_{n+1} - t_n$, $\overline{u}_i^{n+1} = u(\overline{x}_i^{n+1})$ and this is the variable value in the previous time semi-step in the foot of the characteristic line originated at x_i^{n+2} and $\Delta x = x_{i+1} - x_i = \frac{1}{\kappa+1}$, where κ is even. The same characteristic line permits obtaining $\overline{\overline{u}}_i^n$ in the previous semi-step.

Since u_i^{n+2}, where n is even, a numerical approximation for u in (x_i, t_{n+2}), and using a difference operator L, $L_h u_i^n = d \frac{u_{i-1}^n - 2u_i^n + u_{i+1}^n}{\Delta x^2}$, both consecutive semi-steps of the HOPMOC method can be written as:

$$\overline{u}_i^{n+1} = \overline{\overline{u}}_i^n + \delta t \left[\theta_i^n L_h \overline{\overline{u}}_i^n + \theta_i^{n+1} L_h \overline{u}_i^{n+1} \right],$$

$$u_i^{n+2} = \overline{u}_i^{n+1} + \delta t \left[\theta_i^n L_h \overline{u}_i^{n+1} + \theta_i^{n+1} L_h u_i^{n+2} \right],$$

$$\text{for } \theta_i^n = \begin{cases} 1, \text{ if } & n+i \text{ is even,} \\ 0, \text{ if } & n+i \text{ is odd,} \end{cases} \tag{2}$$

and the value $\overline{\overline{u}}_i^n$ is obtained by an interpolation. The values $\overline{x}_i^{n+1}$ and $\overline{\overline{x}}_i^{n+1}$ are obtained by $\overline{x}_i^{n+1} = x_i - v \, \delta t$ and $\overline{\overline{x}}_i^n = x_i - 2v \, \delta t$.

The convergence analysis of the HOPMOC method was presented in [10]. That paper presents the consistency and stability of the method for a convection-diffusion equation. Thus, Lax' theorem guarantees that if the initial value problem is well-posed, then consistency and stability conditions imply the convergence of the numerical method [12]. In [10] it is shown that the HOPMOC

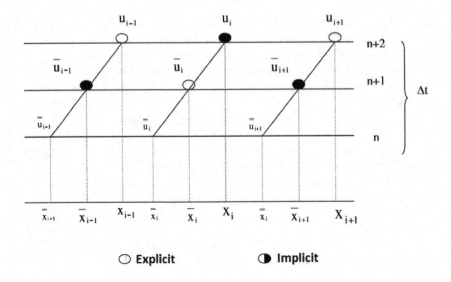

Fig. 1. HopMoc method.

method is unconditionally stable for the convection-diffusion Eq. (1). According to Kischinhevsky [9], this result can be extended to higher dimensions. Figure 1 illustrates the HOPMOC method for one dimensional problem.

For the two dimensional case, two successive steps of group HOPMOC method with four points can be described by Eq. 3.

$$\overline{u}_{i,j}^{n+1} = \overline{\overline{u}}_{i,j}^{n} + \delta t \left[\theta_{i,j}^{n} L_h \overline{\overline{u}}_{i,j}^{n} + \theta_{i,j}^{n+1} L_h \overline{u}_{i,j}^{n+1} \right],$$
$$u_{i,j}^{n+2} = \overline{u}_{i,j}^{n+1} + \delta t \left[\theta_{i,j}^{n} L_h \overline{u}_{i,j}^{n+1} + \theta_{i,j}^{n+1} L_h u_{i,j}^{n+2} \right],$$
$$\text{for } \theta_{i,j}^{n} = \begin{cases} 1, \text{ if } & [i+1]/2 + [j+1]/2 + n \text{ is even,} \\ 0, \text{ if } & [i+1]/2 + [j+1]/2 + n \text{ is odd} \end{cases} \quad (3)$$

Since HOPMOC does not solve any linear system, its parallelization is easily employed because it permits division of the unknowns into two disjoint subsets. Another advantage of HOPMOC is that its computational cost is $O(N)$ per time step.

2.1   1-D HOPMOC Algorithm

The following code is the 1-D HOPMOC algorithm:

```
while (time <= finalTime){
    tempo = (double) (k*deltaT)/2.0;
    for (i = 1 ; i <= N−2 ; i++) {
        x1 = (double) i*deltaX;
        xo = (double) x1 − deltaX;
        xTil = (double) x1 − velX*deltaX;
```

```
       U_new [ i ] = ((x1 − xTil)*U_old [ i −1] +
         (xTil − xo)*U_old [ i ])/( deltaX );
    }
    for ( i = head+1 ; i <= N−2 ; i+=2) {
         U_old [ i ] = alfa *(U_new [ i −1] + U_new [ i +1]) +
         (1 − 2* alfa )*U_new [ i ];
    }
    head = (head+1)
    for ( i = head+1; i <= N−2 ; i+=2) {
         U_old [ i ] = (U_new [ i ] + alfa *U_old [ i −1] + alfa *U_old [ i +1])
                /(1+2* alfa );
    }
}
```

The main loop runs time simulation until it reaches the final time, since its a transient problem. Each time step evaluates the characteristics method and then computes de explicit and implicit operators, alternating which one from the N stencil points are obteined explicitly and implicitly with the variable head that indicates the first point to be evaluated.

We observe that the "while" loop contains 3 independent "for" loops that can be executed in parallel threads on the processor cores. We also observe that the independent loops contains independent floating point vectors that can be executed under simd parallelization paradigm on the processor core units. Therefore, this code can be parallelized and vectorized. Vectorization will permit to exploit full capabilities of one processing unit, while parallelization brings benefits for multithread environments.

3   Computing Environment

All tests shown herein were executed in an 2 sockets Intel Xeon Processor E5-2697 v3 (14 cores, 35 M Cache, 2.60 GHz), with 28 cores and hyperthreading (56 threads), with 96 GB DDR4 RAM. The processor supports Intel AVX2 and the new extension vector processing capability across floating-point and integer data domains. The code was compiled with Intel C++ 15.0.2 version.

The number os points in the stencil for these tests was set to 100000, producing $\Delta x = 10^{-5}$. Other parameters for convection-diffusion equation were: $\Delta t = 10^{-5}$, $\gamma = 10^{-5}$, Final Time $= 0.1$ and $V_x = 5.10^{-5}$.

4   Optimization

Fist we executed the code with the Vtune Amplifier from Intel in order to analyse the algorithm performance bottlenecks on the processors.

The VTune Intel summary analysis results shows that there is a high back-end bound due to memory, in L1 cache level, and core bounds. Figure 2 shows VTune graphics source code and the lines where these bounds occurs. The CPI Rate indicates the latency affecting execution. A high value for CPI indicates that the instruction is taking longer (more clock cycles) than it should to retire from the port. We also observe that the CPI Rate is even higher in line 95,

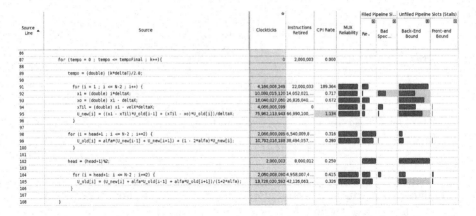

Fig. 2. Unoptimized code analysis - Retire Stalls

probably caused by branch mispredict in line 92, once $x1$ variable is needed to compute. In order to decrease division instruction overhead and data type converting overhead, two changes were applied: (1) Instead of divide part of the calculus by deltaX, we multiply by its inverse (1.0/deltaX) which allows the processor to distribute this calculation among more ports; (2) To avoid data type converting in execution time, all integer values that takes part of U_new and U_old arrays are changed to float, or double, values. The optimized algorithm is presented in the next subsection.

4.1 1-D HOPMOC Algorithm Vectorization

This section describes the 1-D HOPMOC algorithm vectorization. In order to facilitate vectorization of OpenMP codes, Intel extends the set of OpenMP directives by a new set of directives to handle vectorization. The loop header of the associated "for loop" obey the same restrictions as for the existing worksharing constructs. These restrictions enable the OpenMP compiler to determine the iteration space of the loop upfront and distribute it accordingly to fit the vectorization [16].

The following code is the 1-D HOPMOC algorithm vectorized code, based in Intel OpenMP vectorization extension directives:

```
while (time <= finalTime){
  tempo = (double) (k*deltaT)/2.0;

  #pragma vector aligned
  #pragma loop_count max=100000
  #pragma simd vectorlength(4), private(deltaX), linear(i)

  for (i = 1 ; i <= N-2 ; i++) {
    x1 = (double) i*deltaX;
    xo = (double) x1 - deltaX;
    xTil = (double) x1 - velX*deltaX;
    U_new[i] = ((x1 - xTil)*U_old[i-1] + (xTil - xo)*U_old[i])*(1/deltaX);
  }
```

```
#pragma  vector  aligned
#pragma  loop_count  max=50000
#pragma  simd  vectorlength (4),  private(alfa),  linear(i)
#pragma  vector  nontemporal (U_old)

for  (i = head+1 ;  i <= N-2 ;  i+=2) {
    U_old[i] = alfa *(U_new[i-1] + U_new[i+1]) + (1.0 - 2.0* alfa )*U_new[i];
}

head = (head+1)%2;

#pragma  loop_count  max=100000
#pragma  simd  vectorlength (4),  private(alfa),  linear(i)

#pragma  prefetch  *32:64
#pragma  vector  aligned
for  (i = head+1;  i <= N-2 ;  i+=2) {
    U_old[i] = (U_new[i] + alfa *U_old[i-1] + alfa *U_old[i+1]) *
                1/(1.0+2.0* alfa );
}
}
```

Notice that we have used the instruction "pragma vector aligned" on each one of independent "for" loops. While auto-vectorization technology has significantly improved over the years, it is still not possible to vectorize all loops. Although the for construct can help compilers to know where to vectorize, this is not enough because of constraints imposed by the OpenMP specification and because of limitations of compiler technology. To overcome this limitation, Intel presented a new OpenMP directive: the simd directive. This directive allows the programmer to instruct the compiler which loops should be vectorized, and also give some other information by means of the clauses to allow for better vectorization. This directive can also be applied to function declarations so the compiler emits vector-enabled versions of those function to use them from vectorized loops. Intel evaluation with a set of benchmarks shows how the use of this directive can give significant improvements over the auto-vectorizer of a production compiler.

The implementation of the simd directives for OpenMP is based on the existing implementation of Intel Cilk Plus [16]. For each vectorized function with a simd directive, the compiler applies multiversioning and emits several variants of the function to support different vectorization schemes as well as the original scalar code. Creating the scalar code is important not to break (non-vectorized) code that imports symbols from other compilation units. A name-mangling scheme uniquely identifies the created variants so that they can safely be linked into the final executable. At the call site, the compiler searches for the function definition and recreates the mangled name from the usage in the vectorized code. Masking support for a vector function is implemented by adding a hidden formal parameter that contains a boolean. An added if statement only performs the computation of the function when the boolean is true. During vectorization, this boolean is promoted to a vector of booleans to only apply the function to those vector elements for which the mask bit is set to true. When a linear clause is present, the compiler does not promote the parameter to a vector, but instead keeps the scalar parameter. A linear clause directs the compiler to use scalar loads/stores and to assume that data referenced by the linear parameter is stored in memory with the stride specified at the clause (unit stride by default). The compiler can automatically determine the correct value for vector length in most cases. From the data type used in the computation and the target machine instruction set, the compiler can deduce the vector length (e.g., 2 for double-precision with SSE or 8 for single-precision with AVX). Specifying a vectorlength that is a multiple of a vector length instructs the compiler to use double-pumping or quad-pumping, that is, to fuse multiple physical registers into a single virtual register.

To accomplished the results shown above, some additional issues had to be considered: first, one can force vectorization with #pragma simd that instructs the compiler to execute one instruction with multiple data simultaneously, inside the vector unit; secondly, #pragma vector nontemporal is used to instruct the compiler to use streaming store for U_OLD array, since there are no data dependencies; the last issue regards on data latency which can be minimized hinting the compiler to generate data prefetch.

Finally, we notice that the execution time from the original code decreases from 55,445 s to 29,642 s on the vectorized optimized.

Next section show how parallelism can make use of multithread environment, reducing even more the total elapsed time.

4.2   Parallelization

For many years, OpenMP has been the model of choice for programming on shared memory multiprocessors within the high-performance community. Although OpenMP is promoted as being easy to use and allows incremental parallelization of codes, naive implementations frequently yield poor performance. In practice, as with other models such as MPI, the same care and attention should be exercised over algorithm and hardware details when programming with OpenMP.

In OpenMP applications, programmers extract parallelism by using a series of pragmas that annotate specific types of parallelism. The omp parallel pragma annotates regions of code that are executed by all worker threads in parallel.

With each worker thread having a unique ID, the programmer can then assign a unique subset of the problem to each worker thread. In addition to parallel sections, many applications contain loops in which every iteration is independent of every other. For this type of parallelism, commonly referred as DOALL parallelism, OpenMP offers the pragma omp for easy annotation. Used inside omp parallel code blocks, omp for allows participating worker threads to divide available loop iterations using one of three different loop scheduling policies: Static, Dynamic and Guided.

As with many other runtime libraries, programmers have little information regarding the actual management cost of parallelism. There seems to be, however, the general idea that dynamic management of parallelism is more expensive than static arrangements, and that coarse-grain parallelism is preferred over fine-grain parallelism in order to hide runtime library overheads. The work from [3] shows that for both static and dynamic schedules, the overall contribution of the runtime library increases with increasing core counts. For static, barrier costs from implicit synchronization at the end of parallel loops account for a significant portion of the runtime execution. For dynamic, lock contention becomes a major bottleneck with increasing core counts. Thus, as more worker threads attempt to grab work, synchronization overheads become significant, eventually overshadowing any parallelism performance gains. Increasing synchronization overheads decreases the performance potential of applications, even when the annotated parallelism in the applications is able to scale well. At low core counts (2 to 8 cores), most of the overhead comes from the use of various library runtime procedures. At higher core counts, synchronization overheads start becoming significant. Excessive task creation can induce significant overhead if task granularity is not sufficiently big (approximately 100 K cycles), which is the task granularity size of our performance evaluation tests.

4.3   Data Parallelization

This subsection describes the 1-D HOPMOC algorithm Data Parallelization. In order to keep to load balanced we divided the data domain by the number of threads and keep the number of threads equal to the number of cores of the processors. This strategy allows the code to be executed in all available cores in the processor, and to keep the data distributed evenly within the cores. The following code is the 1-D HOPMOC algorithm Data Parallelization code:

```
while (time <= finalTime){

    #pragma loop_count max=100000
    #pragma simd vectorlength(4), private(alfa), linear(i)

    #pragma prefetch *32:64
    #pragma vector aligned
    #pragma omp for private(i)
    for (i = head+1; i <= N-2 ; i+=2) {
        U_old[i] = (U_new[i] + alfa*U_old[i-1] + alfa*U_old[i+1]) *
                    1/(1.0+2.0*alfa);
    }
}
```

While the simd construct vectorizes sequential loops, the simd for construct combines the semantics of the for and simd constructs in a single construct. It vectorizes a loop and distributes it across the binding thread set.The combined constructs go beyond mere syntactical sugar. The combined simd for slightly changes the semantics of the optional chunk size of the scheduling clause. In simd worksharing constructs, the chunk size refers to the chunk size after vectorization has been applied. That is, a loop chunk is created after the loop has been distributed across the simd registers. In order to improve the load balancing of the system, we have to evaluate the performance for the additional vectorization clauses: Data Sharing Clauses, Controlling the Vector Length, Induction Variables and Data Alignment.

Data Sharing Clauses. All OpenMP data-sharing clauses are available to control the visibility and sharing of variables for vectorized loops. The private clause creates an uninitialized vector for the given variables. The firstprivate clause promotes variables to private vectors that are initialized with values from outside the loop. With lastprivate, a private vector is created and the variable's value in the last loop iteration is retained. The reduction clause creates a private copy of the variable and horizontally aggregates partial values of a vector into a global, scalar reduction result.

Controlling the Vector Length. The default vector length can be specified through the vectorlength and vectorlengthfor clauses. If the compiler cannot determine the correct vector length (e.g., due to loop-carried dependencies), the programmer may use vectorlength to enable vectorization. The value for vectorlength must be of an integral compile-time constant and depends on the data type used for computation and the distance of the loop-carried dependency (if any). It must also be a power of two (e.g., 2, 4, 8). For instance, a loop working on double values would select 4 as the vector length when compiling for a processor with support for Intel AVX. The vectorlengthfor clause helps identify the correct vector length for a given data type. It accepts a data type of the base language as its argument and automatically chooses the vector length to fit the machine architecture.

Induction Variables. Induction variables are variables whose value linearly depends on the loop counter of a loop. With the linear clause, a programmer can specify a set of variables that shall be considered induction variables across loop iterations. For each variable, the linear clause accepts the identifier and an increment. The increment can either be a compile-time constant or a variable. When the compiler vectorizes the loop, the compiler generates vectors that contain the induction values for the current loop chunk and makes sure that the vector is updated accordingly along the loop iteration space.

Data Alignment. Data alignment is important since most platforms can load aligned data much faster than unaligned data. This especially applies to vectors. Yet, compilers are in general not able to detect the alignment properties of data across all modules of a program. Compilers, thus, have to react conservatively and emit code that uses only unaligned loads and stores. Hence, the align clause explicitly provide this knowledge to the compiler.

Forced Vectorization. The simd construct implies that the associated loop or function is always vectorized by the OpenMP compiler. If the compiler cannot vectorize the code for some reason (e.g., a too complex code pattern), it should abort compilation and emit a diagnostic message to inform the programmer. This can help programmers avoid an unexpected performance behavior and reduce the (performance) debugging effort.

4.4   DATA Parallelization Performance Evaluation

This section presents the performance evaluation from domain decomposition parallel approach.

In order to evaluate the parallel performance we are presenting three performance evaluation indices for the parallel model: speedup, time saving ratio and efficiency.

The speedup formula is as $S_n = T/T_n$. Where T is the serial computing time and T_n is the computation time with n parallel threads.

The efficiency formula is $E_n = S_n/n$. Where n is the number of parallel threads.

The time, speedup, and efficiency required for calculation are as shown in Fig. 3.

Threads	Time (sec)	Speedup	Parallel Efficiency
1	24,27	1	100%
2	12,31	1,972	98,578%
4	6,36	3,816	95,401%
8	3,37	7,202	90,022%
16	2,15	11,288	70,552%
32	1,9	12,774	39,918%

Fig. 3. Speedup analysis

As shown in Fig. 3 (1) The computation time reduces as the number of threads increases. For example, for the single thread with simd optimizations the computation is 24,27 s, but required only 1,9 s with 56 threads. The parallel model therefore plays an important role in accelerating the model operation period. (2) The speedup factor increases with the number of threads. In Scheme 3, for example, speedup factors of 1.9, 3.8, 7.2, 11.2 and 12,7 were achieved with 2, 4, 8, 16, and 32 threads, respectively, demonstrating great extendibility. (3) The efficiency reduces as the number of threads increases. In Scheme 2, for example, the efficiency drops from 98,57 % with two threads to just 39.9 % with 56 threads, which indicates that the overall model performance is deteriorating.

For a fixed number of threads, the computation time, speedup, and efficiency increases with the number of grid cells.

As the 24,27 s became 1,9 s, the number of calculations increases, which led to the increase in simulation time. The speedup and efficiency also improves as the number of grid cells increases, although the increase is slow, demonstrating that the parallel model performs better with an increased calculation load.

Figure 3 illustrates the speedup factor for different thread numbers. As shown in the figure, the speedup increases as the number thread increases, but the startup, assignment, switching, and revocation of threads consumes time. Thus, with any increase in thread number, the system overheads increases, and the computation time that can be saved reduces. This leads to an overall decline in model performance, and thus the relative increase in the speedup factor is reduced.

4.5   Work Parallelization

This section presents the performance evaluation from functional decomposition parallel approach. We can exploit one more level of parallelism, the parallelism of functions. Since the three main steps of HOPMOC Method are almost independent, requiring only a synchronization mechanism amon them, these steps can be parallelized too. In this sense, we can achieve two types of parallelism in the same implementation: (1) data and (2) task parallelism. The idea behind this strategy is to split spatial points of domain among a pool of threads and which of these threads is broken into more three child threads that will compute one of the HOPMOC steps.

The following code is the 1-D HOPMOC algorithm Task Parallelization code:

```
while (time <= finalTime){
    tempo = (double) (k*deltaT)/2.0;
    #pragma omp sections
      {
        #pragma omp section
          {
            #pragma omp for
            for (i = 1 ; i <= N-2 ; i++) {
              //Characteristics Method
            }
          }
        #pragma omp section
          {
          #pragma omp for
          for (i = head+1 ; i <= N-2 ; i+=2) {
            //Explicit Operator
          }
          }
        #pragma omp section
          {
            #pragma omp for
            for (i = head+1; i <= N-2 ; i+=2) {
              //Implicit Operator
            }
          }
      }
}
```

It's necessary to enable the nested parallelism mechanism with omp_set_nested (1) in order to permit a thread to create other threads. In each section we put a HOPMOC task and which one splits its own data into data parallelism with #pragma omp for. A synchronization scheme avoids that task 2 operates over data not performed by task 1 and the same for task 3 over task2.

We evaluate the performance for number of threads equal to the number of cores, i.e. 12 threads and we improved the speed-up up to 3 times faster than the data parallelism approach and we intend to further investigate for a higher number of threads.

5   Conclusion and Future Work

This paper describes the study of a vectorized and parallelized implementation of a Numerical Method for convection-diffusion equations to solve parabolic equations with convective dominance on a Intel Xeon Haswell architecture.

Numerical results show the gain of performance up to 2 times per core when compared to sequential version for solving a convective-diffusion equation through a vectorized code implementation.

This work also presents a further performance improvement, up to 11 times for 12 tasks, through the implementation of a data parallel code on the "vectorized code" and even better performance improvement, up to 3 times, through the implementation of a task parallelization on the "data parallel vectorized code".

We conclude that adding vectorizes and parallelizes data and task implementations can improve our numerical method code up 36 times on the Xeon Haswell architecture

As a forthcoming work, we plan to extend our study for task and data paralelization on both Xeon and Xeon Phi architecture.

These studies are first steps to implement HOPMOC numerical method on cluster in order to scale the application in a heterogeneous environment.

It's proposed that these features to be investigated combined to MPI, to try a better performance increasing for HOPMOC. Additionally, a study on the impact of the different domain partitions in the final distributed execution time is to be performed. The new features available at MPI 3.0, such as multi thread MPI processes should be considered. An important trend to be considered in multicore/manycore programming is the merge of OpenMP and the vectorized code. As present in [10] the phase of interpolation to calculate the value of foot of characteristic introduces some error in the method. Total Variation Diminishing (TVD) techniques are used to reduced the error of convective term interpolation [13], we will investigate if TVD techniques applied to HOPMOC method can be reduces the interpolation error.

Acknowledgments. This project was partially supported by cooperation agreement between LNCC and Intel Corporation.

References

1. Kischinhevsky, M.: An Operator Splitting for Optimal Message-passing Computation of Parabolic Equation with Hyperbolic Dominance. SIAM Annual Meeting, Missouri (1996)
2. Boonkkamp, J.H.M.T.J., Verwer, J.G.: On the odd-even hopscotch scheme for the numerical integration of time-dependent partial differential equations. Appl. Num. Math. **3**(1), 183–193 (1987)
3. Hansen, J.P., Matthey, T., Sørevik, T.: A parallel split operator method for the time dependent Schrödinger equation. In: Dongarra, J., Laforenza, D., Orlando, S. (eds.) EuroPVM/MPI 2003. LNCS, vol. 2840, pp. 503–510. Springer, Heidelberg (2003)
4. Yanenko, N.N.: The Method of Fractional Steps. Springer, New York (1970)
5. Li, D., Zhou, Z., Wang, Q.: A hybrid MPI/OpenMP based on DDM for large-scale partial differential equations. In: IEEE 11th International Conference on Trust, Security and Privacy in Computing and Communications, Liverpool, pp. 1839–1843 (2012)
6. Jin, H., Jespersen, D., Mehrotra, P., Biswas, R., Huang, L., Chapman, B.: High performance computing using MPI and OpenMP on multi-core parallel systems. Parallel Comput. **37**(9), 562–575 (2011)
7. Mininni, P.D., Rosenberg, D., Reddy, R., Poquet, A.: A hybrid MPI-OpenMP scheme for scalable parallel pseudospectral computations for fluid turbulence. Parallel Comput. **37**, 316–326 (2011)
8. Kirk, D.B., Hwu, W.W.: Programming Massively Parallel Processors: A Hands-on Approach. Elsevier Inc., Philadelphia (2010)
9. Kischinhevsky, M.: A spatially decoupled alternating direction procedure for convection-diffusion equations. In: Proceedings of the XXth CILAMCE-Iberian Latin American Congress on Numerical Methods in Engineearing (1999)
10. Oliveira, S., Gonzaga, S.L., Kischinhevsky, M.: Convergence analysis of the HOPMOC method. Int. J. Comput. Math. **86**, 1375–1393 (2009)
11. Cabral, F.L.: HOPMOC methods to solve convection-diffusion equations and its parallel implementation (in Portuguese). Master thesis, Instituto de Computação/Universidade Federal Fluminense, Brasil (2001)
12. Richtmyer, R.D., Morton, K.W.: Difference Methods for Initial-Value Problems Interscience. Interscience, New York (1967)
13. Harten, A.: On a class of high resolution total-variation-stable finite-difference schemes. SIAM J. Numer. Anal. **21**, 1–23 (1984)
14. Rabeinsefner, R., Hager, G., Jost, G.: Hybrid MPI/OpenMP parallel programming on clusters of molti-core SMP nodes. In: 2009 17th Euromicro International Conference on Parallel, Distributed and Network-based Processing, pp. 427–436 (2009)
15. Cluster OpemMP for Intel Compilers. http://software.intel.com/en-us/articles/cluster-openmp-for-intel-compilers
16. Klemm, M., Duran, A., Tian, X., Saito, H., Caballero, D., Martorell, X.: Extending OpenMP* with vector constructs for modern multicore SIMD architectures. In: Chapman, B.M., Massaioli, F., Müller, M.S., Rorro, M. (eds.) IWOMP 2012. LNCS, vol. 7312, pp. 59–72. Springer, Heidelberg (2012)
17. Cabral, F.L., Osthoff, C., Kischinhevsky, M., Brandão. D.: Hybrid MPI/OpenMP/OpenACC Implementations for the Solution of Convection-Diffusion Equations with the HOPMOC Method. In: Proceedings of XXIV International Conference on Computational Science and Its Applications (2014)

Parallel Performance Analysis of a Regional Numerical Weather Prediction Model in a Petascale Machine

Roberto Pinto Souto[1]($\boxtimes$), Pedro Leite da Silva Dias[1], and Franck Vigilant[2]

[1] National Laboratory for Scientific Computing (LNCC), 333 Avenida Getulio Vargas, Petrópolis 25651-075, Brazil
{rpsouto,pldsdias}@lncc.br
http://www.lncc.br
[2] Atos/Bull Center for Excellence in Parallel Programming (CEPP),
1 Rue de Provence, 38432 Échirolles, France
franck.vigilant@atos.net
http://www.bull.com

Abstract. This paper presents the parallel performance achieved by a regional model of numerical weather prediction (NWP), running on thousands of computing cores in a petascale supercomputing system. It was obtained good scalability, running with up to 13440 cores, distributed in 670 nodes. These results enables this application to solve large computational challenges, such as perform weather forecast at very high spatial resolution.

Keywords: Parallel performance analysis · Numerical weather prediction · Petascale supercomputing

1 Introduction

One of the scientific applications that require more processing power is the numerical weather prediction (NWP). There is huge amount of data to be processed in order to feed the equations that advance in time the status of the atmosphere.

Several factors contribute to configure the high computational cost of an NWP. For example, the larger the geographical domain and the number of days of forecast, greater the amount of data to be processed.

Moreover, remaining unchanged the domain and the model integration time (the number of days of forecast), can vary both the number of points in the discretized grid domain, as the number of the steps performed during integration. The former defines the spatial resolution, and the last gives the temporal resolution, or the time-step of the forecast. The larger the resolution, more processing will be performed for the same spatial domain.

The use of high performance computing resources becomes mandatory in this type of application, especially the use of distributed memory machines. For high

© Springer International Publishing Switzerland 2015
C. Osthoff et al. (Eds.): CARLA 2015, CCIS 565, pp. 145–150, 2015.
DOI: 10.1007/978-3-319-26928-3_11

spatial resolution the larger number of grid points may lead to memory restrictions because the domain decomposition may, eventually reach the maximum memory available for each processing node.

It is therefore important that the NWP has enough scalability to run on a maximum number of processing nodes, to make feasible the weather forecast for the defined spatial and temporal resolutions.

2   BRAMS Developments

The numerical model of prediction BRAMS (Brazilian developments on the Regional Atmospheric Modeling System) [1,2] is a regional-scale model, developed at INPE/CPTEC (National Institute for Space Research/Center for Weather Forecasts and Climate Studies), based on the model RAMS (Regional Atmospheric Modeling System) [3,4]. In BRAMS were introduced several changes in the source code of RAMS, which yielded a more realistic description of tropical processes including the precipitation, land/surface interaction and the role of aerosols in the short wave radiation.

Another important feature introduced in BRAMS was the parallel implementation with MPI [5], which had not been done in RAMS. The parallel strategy employed is the domain decomposition, where the atmosphere state advancement of each domain partition is assigned to an MPI process different. This parallel strategy follows the master-slave pattern, where the master node makes the decomposition of the domain, and sends to the slave nodes the data necessary to processing their respective partition.

This worked fine for order of tens of computational nodes, with spatial resolution around 20 km in the domain of operational forecasting of INPE/CPTEC, which covers the whole of Brazil, and almost all of South America, as shown by the gray area in Fig. 1.

By adopting resolution of 10 km, running in the order of hundreds of processing nodes, the memory used has exceeded the amount available in the master node, occurring memory paging, resulting in a performance bottleneck due to the master node.

One new implementation was then proposed [6,7], by eliminating the master node. All nodes read the data and make its own domain decomposition. The code in this version performs with good scalability with hundreds of nodes, under a resolution of 10 km

To achieve the target to run the model with 5 km resolution in a feasible time, it was necessary to make BRAMS perform on thousands of processing nodes.

But, in that resolution, the amount of memory per process reaches about 3.9 GB. Then, nodes with 32 GB of RAM, such as the machine of INPE/CPTEC, could be executed with up to 8 MPI processes, limiting the scalability of the application, since each node has 24 cores ($2\times$ AMD Opteron Magny-Cours/12-core, 2.1 GHz).

This problem occurs because of memory reservation made for arrays in the early of forecast, even if not fully utilized. The solution found was the use of

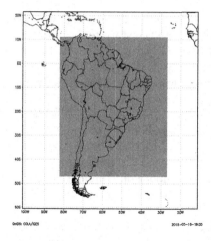

Fig. 1. Domain of operational weather forecast of INPE/CPTEC.

dynamic allocation of arrays, reducing the amount of memory per process to about 1.18 GB [8]. Thus, it was possible to use all 24 cores of the nodes, without exceeding the available RAM in each node.

3   Results

In order to perform the parallel performance analysis of BRAMS model, version 5.0 was used, and the case study was the operational spatial domain of INPE/CPTEC, described in Sect. 2.

The grid of the corresponding domain in BRAMS contains 1360 and 1480 points in the zonal and meridional directions, respectively. The same grid is repeated in 45 vertical levels.

These values correspond respectively to parameters NNXP, NNYP and NNZP shown in Table 1. The spatial resolution used was 5 km, in both directions, horizontal and vertical (DELTAX = 5000 and DELTAY = 5000).

Table 1. BRAMS parameters

Parameter	Value
NNXP	1360 points
NNYP	1480 points
NNZP	45 levels
DELTAX	5000 m
DELTAY	5000 m
TIMMAX	1 h
DTLONG	10 s

The integration time, i.e., the prediction time was one hour (TIMMAX = 1). The BRAMS was set to update the state the atmosphere every 10 s, and this is the time-step value (DTLONG = 10). Therefore, for a 1-h weather forecast, or 3600 s, there are 360 time-steps, lasting 10 s each.

The parallel executions were made in the Tier-0 machine of the Brazilian High Performance System, the SDumont cluster (an ATOS/BULL machine). This machine is composed of 756 nodes, interconnected by FDR Infiniband in a fat-tree topology, sharing a parallel file system of 1.7 Petabytes (Lustre). Each node has 2 CPU Intel Xeon E5-2695v2 (12-core, 2.4 GHz) with 64 GB of RAM. There are therefore a total of 18144 computational cores.

From the total of the 756 nodes of SDumont cluster, 198 nodes contains two GPUs NVIDIA K40 (396 GPU boards), and other 54 nodes have 2 Intel Xeon Phi (MIC 108 boards).

The overall potential processing (Rpeak) of the whole cluster, including every installed parallel architectures, is about 1.1 Petaflop. In the ocasion of acceptance tests of the machine, done in ATOS/BULL factory, the High Performance Linpack (HPL) [9] reaches nearly 0.8 Petaflop.

The compiler used was the Intel Fortran version 15.0.2, and the distribution of MPI was bullx MPI, a Bull implementation based on OpenMPI.

BRAMS is executed in two phases. In the first one, input data of topography, vegetation, soil moisture, besides the boundary condition, are interpolated to the specified resolution in the grid. Moreover, in this phase is made the domain decomposition, distributed among all cores.

In the second phase is where then performed the weather forecast, i.e., the status of atmosphere is iteratively updated by the model in periodic intervals (time-steps), until is reached the total integration time (1-h, 24-h, 48-h, and so on).

Parallel executions of BRAMS were made from 1024 cores (64 nodes) up to 13400 cores (670 nodes), for 1-h of integration time. Table 2 lists the runtime obtained, as well as both the ideal and achieved speed-up, and also the reached parallel efficiency.

It is observed that the scalability of BRAMS was quite satisfactory, since for the maximum number of cores used, the parallel efficiency was 78 %. In the other parallel executions, from 1024 up to 10320 cores, efficiency was higher than 90 % or close to this value.

It is important to repair that, as longer is the weather forecast, is less significant the time of the first phase, regarding to total model time. For operational purposes, the relevant runtime for performance evaluation is due to integration of the model, since usually is done a 7-day (168-h) weather forecast.

Table 3 lists the runtime obtained, achieved speed-up and parallel efficiency, considering the total runtime, not only the integration runtime for 168-h weather forecast, by extrapolating 1-h of integration.

Asymptotically, the overall performance of the model tends to the parallel performance of the integration phase.

Table 2. Parallel performance of BRAMS in SDumont for 1-h weather forecast: analysis based only in integration runtime of the model

Nodes	Cores per node[a]	Total cores	Total time(s)	Init. time(s)	Integ. time(s)	Linear speed-up	Obtained speed-up	Efficiency
64	16	1024	977	298	679			
128	16	2048	652	304	348	2.00	1.95	0.98
256	16	4096	510	330	180	4.00	3.77	0.94
512	16	8192	778	681	97	8.00	7.03	0.88
645	16	10320	665	588	77	10.08	8.83	0.88
670	20	13400	935	868	67	13.09	10.14	0.78

[a] *Physical cores. Hyper-Threading not activated*

Table 3. Parallel performance of BRAMS in SDumont for 7-day (168-h) weather forecast, by extrapolating 1-h runtime: analysis based in total runtime of the model

Nodes	Cores per node	Total cores	Total time(s)	Init. time(s)	Integ. time(s)	Linear speed-up	Obtained speed-up	Efficiency
64	16	1024	114452	298	114154			
128	16	2048	58702	304	58398	2.00	1.95	0.97
256	16	4096	30590	330	30260	4.00	3.74	0.94
512	16	8192	16913	681	16232	8.00	6.77	0.85
645	16	10320	13519	588	12931	10.08	8.47	0.84
670	20	13400	12123	868	11254	13.09	9.44	0.72

This efficiency is greater than that obtained in the INPE/CPTEC machine, where efficiency is 58 % for 9600 cores, compared execution time in 1200 cores [8].

The threshold used for that the development code goes into operation, is 20 min a day of integration (24-h weather forecast) [8]. However, by extrapolating the runtime with 13400 cores, from 1-h to 24-h weather forecast, the estimated runtime is 1608 s, or 26.8 min. As comparison, in the INPE/CPTEC machine, using 9600 cores, the runtime was 1180 s, or 19.7 min, for 24-h integration.

4 Final Remarks

According to analysis of the results, it was observed that the BRAMS has very good scalability in SDumont cluster, It is higher than that obtained in the operating cluster INPE/CPTEC. Further study is needed to explain the better scalability.

The fact that the two clusters use different interconnecting networks, also with different topologies, may indicate the possible causes. The SDumont cluster has Infiniband FDR interconnection network with fat-tree topology, while the cluster INPE/CPTEC, a Cray XE6, has proprietary interconnection network with toroidal topology.

This good scalability, enables the BRAMS as an application with great potential for use of SDumont cluster in order to solve large computational challenges.

During the first period of tests of the SDumont cluster, as soon as it installed on LNCC campus, will be made new executions with BRAMS, adopting spatial resolution higher than 5 km, reaching up to 1 km resolution.

Although the domain of the region to be used is smaller than the one used in this paper, the problem of size in number of grid points increases significantly. This will lead to a greater amount of memory required by MPI process.

It is expected that, either because of good relations of 2.7 GB per core, or then due to the large number of available nodes, the SDumont cluster will be able to handle weather forecasts with increasing spatial resolution.

Another research, is the use of accelerators, such as massively parallel architectures, such as GPU and MIC.

It is believed that the time-steps that run the physics of prediction have good speed-up potential with the use of these architectures.

Acknowledgments. This project is supported by FINEP Brazilian funding agency (process number 01.14.192.00). The authors would like also to thank to ATOS/BULL for make available its computing resources in order to adapt BRAMS to run in SDumont cluster.

References

1. INPE/CPTEC Brazilian developments on the regional atmospheric modelling system (1999)
2. Freitas, S.R., Longo, K.M., Silva Dias, M.A.F., Chatfield, R., Silva Dias, P., Artaxo, P., Andreae, M.O., Grell, G., Rodrigues, L.F., Fazenda, A., Panetta, J.: Atmos. Chem. Phys. **9**(8), 2843–2861 (2009)
3. Pielke, R., Cotton, W., Walko, R., Tremback, C., Lyons, W., Grasso, L., Nicholls, M., Moran, M., Wesley, D., Lee, T., Copeland, J.: Meteorol. Atmos. Phys. **49**(1–4), 69–91 (1992)
4. Cotton, W.R., Pielke Sr., R., Walko, R., Liston, G., Tremback, C., Jiang, H., McAnelly, R., Harrington, J., Nicholls, M., Carrio, G., et al.: Meteorol. Atmos. Phys. **82**(1-4), 5–29 (2003)
5. Gropp, W., Lusk, E., Doss, N., Skjellum, A.: Parallel Comput. **22**(6), 789–828 (1996)
6. Fazenda, A.L., Panetta, J., Navaux, P., Rodrigues, L.F., Katsurayama, D.M., Motta, L.F.: Anais do X Simpósio em Sistemas Computacionais (WSCAD-SCC), pp. 27–34 (2009)
7. Fazenda, A.L., Panetta, J., Katsurayama, D.M., Rodrigues, L.F., Motta, L.F., Navaux, P.O.: Int. J. High Perform. Syst. Architect. **3**(2–3), 87–97 (2011)
8. Fazenda, A.L., Rodrigues, E.R., Tomita, S.S., Panetta, J., Mendes, C.L.: 2012 13th Symposium on IEEE Computer Systems (WSCAD-SSC), pp. 126–132 (2012)
9. Petitet, A., Whaley, R.C., Dongarra, J., Cleary, A.: HPL - a portable implementation of the High-Performance linpack benchmark for Distributed-Memory computers

Author Index

Printed in the United States
By Bookmasters